A Crisis of Trust

Stuart Wheeler

© The Bruges Group 2010
ISBN: 978-0-9564614-0-7

Published in February 2010 by
The Bruges Group, 227 Linen Hall, 162-168 Regent Street, London W1B 5TB
www.brugesgroup.com

Bruges Group publications are not intended to represent a corporate view of European
and international developments. Contributions are chosen on the basis of their intellectual rigour
and their ability to open up new avenues for debate.

Acknowledgements

It is not secret corruption which is the danger in politics. The forms of corruption to be feared are not those which would be denied, or would be a cause of shame, if they were publicly exposed. The really dangerous forms of political corruption are those which are open and acknowledged, which, if hon. members like, are part of the system.

– Enoch Powell (20 December 1971)

My thanks go to the Bruges Group for publishing this pamphlet. And to Professor Tim Congdon, Ruth Lea, Ewen Stewart, Dr John Adamson, Chris Mounsey, Dr Lee Rotherham, Yvonne Carlton, Clare Steiner, Richard Thoburn, Amelia Bauerly and Barry Legg for their assistance. The opinions expressed are my own.

Much of my treatment of the expenses scandal consists of my disagreement with the cross-party support for the recommendations in the 12th Report of the Committee on Standards in Public Life [CSPL, 12th Report, Cm 7724]. The Committee is currently chaired by the distinguished public servant, Sir Christopher Kelly, and I refer to the Committee's findings throughout as *Kelly*. Sir Christopher's sincerity and manifest hard work are in no way to be questioned. Sadly, however, I disagree with many of the conclusions of his report.

1.
Worthy of their position?

Being a member of parliament is not just a vocation for the man or woman fortunate enough to be called to do it. Electing a person to sit in the Commons is the highest trust the British people can place in someone. Too many MPs have proved unworthy of it. Moreover the party system, by reducing private members to state-funded obedient servants, has severely damaged the House of Commons.

Damage to our political system

Let me turn to the great expenses scandal of 2009. It has shown that trends which started a generation ago have had all the ill effects we should have foreseen. We risk permanently damaging our political system. Essential reforms are not being made. So the disastrous behaviour that has so diminished the standing of Westminster will be able to continue. If we pursue the course which cross-party consensus now suggests, we shall do even greater harm to British democracy.

Further decline is likely

Can the situation really deteriorate further? Well, no party took any action on expenses until the truth came out. Together, the political class defeated the few brave MPs and outsiders who drew attention to the abuses, and called for change. Only the intervention of a free press (however imperfect) brought things into the open. My view is that the defensive, reactive programme of the three main parties and their endorsement of the Kelly Report[1] will, far from solving the problem, perpetuate and even entrench it.

Kelly Report inadequate

We have to remember that the parties endorsing the proposed reforms, whether their own or *Kelly's*, are the same ones that so desperately need to be reformed. Until the intervention of *The Daily Telegraph*[2], this political class resisted every attempt at change. They defended every privilege and reward they had built up.

Exposure, reasoned arguments and even proof of guilt all failed to convince MPs of any party that the system they had made for themselves was intolerable.

Inadequate punishment

Worse still is the 'fate' of those who have been caught. The only sanction has been that once exposed, they must pay back what they now agree they should never have had. Beyond this? Nothing. True, several dozen MPs – mostly those who were anyway likely to be defeated at the polls or whom their respective party leaderships had no political interest in preserving – have announced that they will no longer stand for re-election, or have been informed by their parties that they will no longer be allowed to. But one question is whether the House itself should have expelled them, because it seems that those MPs most valued by their leaders get away with it.

From soldiers to welfare claimants, any other class of publicly paid individuals – had they behaved as MPs have – would have suffered far harsher penalties than MPs have imposed upon themselves. I shall return to the question of what MPs *should* be paid. But although MPs have pointed to the private sacrifices many of them have undoubtedly made by choosing public service, had they cheated on their expenses in an 'ordinary' job, they might well have earned themselves dismissal or worse. *Kelly's* sanctions, to which I will return, amount to little that will deter MPs, which is a great pity as many of the offenders will be in the next parliament.

The public's contempt

The revelations of the last year have of course diminished public confidence in politicians. I shall have more to say about the actions of the party leaderships, and how they have given themselves the power to decide who their candidates are.

At its founding, the United States learned much from us, and it is time for us to repay the compliment. American politicians show admirable independence for many reasons, but especially because they are not ruled by centralised party machines. They are ruled by those who elected them – who are also those who selected them. Proper reform of parliament requires MPs, and those who aspire to be MPs, to be much freer from the tyranny of their parties. MPs must be able to question those who lead them.

All one political class

MPs have, in the last few decades, become a class apart. Recently the public's feeling that MPs are irrelevant has grown to out-and-out contempt. Not long ago,

Britain could claim a more socially representative and diverse legislature than any other western democracy. This was mainly achieved by the Labour party. Elsewhere, rich men, party servants and, inevitably, lawyers, dominated both continental parliaments and those in the New World, regardless of nominal party affiliation. We were different. Every accent was to be heard in the Commons, every class spoke up.

Now, an ever more uniform political class rules. MPs are increasingly drawn from political backgrounds. Where once parliament contained many with experience of the world, it now increasingly consists of men and women who have done nothing but work in politics, or dependent spheres such as lobbying and the political media. We look likely to find ourselves with more and more such politicians. Restoring respect for parliament will need the election of many MPs with experience of the outside world. And these MPs will have to be free to display independence from their parties.

Much of my argument about how trust can best be restored to parliament amounts to a rejection of *Kelly*, in spite of the fact that it has been agreed to almost without exception by the three largest parties. One perhaps counter-intuitive point, I believe, is that MPs *must* remain responsible for their own pay and allowances. That is the only way *we*, the electors, can retain a democratic say on that subject.

The system's fault, even more than MPs'

While there is no reason to suppose that Tony Blair and Gordon Brown were themselves corrupt, their governments are chiefly to blame for the expenses scandal, by giving MPs the most easily corruptible regime the state has ever seen. The polls seem to show that the public thinks much the same thing. So I have devoted considerable attention to our likely next government.

Here the tragedy is that though Labour created the system, the Tories seem very happy to let it go on. When I talk about some of what we have discovered in the last year, my intention is only illustrative. There are many, many more examples. We need to appreciate what leading members of Mr Cameron's party apparently have not. It would of course help if at least members of the cabinet and shadow cabinet revealed what they did before The Daily Telegraph was able to start telling us the truth.

At this point, I should perhaps say something about myself. I came to politics late in life. I did so by giving money to causes I believed in, not because I wanted anything from them. Though I am well off, and lucky enough to have enjoyed an excellent education, I have no desire for parliament ever again to be open only to those with money. MPs must be paid enough to ensure that political participation is not restricted to those with private means.

But although it is one thing to go into politics rich, it is quite another to come out of it richer still. The decline in standards and the failure of our elected representatives to know better are deplorable. Being an MP is a great privilege. If I fail to convince you of anything else, I hope that you will at least agree that untrustworthy MPs cost the country much more than just money. My biggest purpose in this pamphlet is to explain why I fear that the parties do not intend to behave in a way which really would regain our trust.

Pay and allowances in the past

Going back in history it seems that MPs were relatively slow to feather their own nests – although that may be due more to lack of opportunity than greed. Medieval parliaments generally met for brief periods, and MPs were expected to find their own accommodation at their own expense. As payments were very small or non-existent, almost the only financial perk available to members of the Commons was the prospect, if they were meeting near the itinerant royal court, of a free dinner in the hall of a nearby palace. This system remained for the most part unchanged until the early seventeenth century.

At the time of the Civil War, as now, it was the cost of maintaining a second home that provided MPs with an obvious pretext for dipping into public funds. From 1645 the Commons introduced its first housing allowance: £4 per week for MPs who could not use their main house in their constituency and needed to pay for accommodation so that they could go about the 'Service of the House'.[3] Where benefits were not paid in cash, they could be paid in kind. Vacant properties in state control were assigned to cronies of the prevailing party in the Commons, with little or no scrutiny of the arrangements, even by the House itself.

The immediate casualty of this system of manipulable financial rewards was, as ever, the independence and the public standing of individual MPs. One prolific 1640s journalist commented that MPs had become automata who had been 'taught to speak Aye or No' and to give their votes 'at certain hours by direction, just like Cheapside clock-strikers'.[4] Backbenchers, it was alleged, had simply become 'voting instruments': 'those state-catamites, upon whom any votes whatsoever may be begotten'.

To some, the whole party system was a sham, presenting a series of fake disagreements on principle to the public, while in reality the party 'grandees' were at one in their readiness to milk the cash cows of the kingdom's Exchequer, and to co-operate with one another in doing so. Loyalty was up for sale, bought by conferring 'something of advantage upon those that are subservient to them, as five pounds a week' – the increased housing allowance – 'or some petty employment'.[5]

Co-operation to conceal

MPs worked hard to keep such arrangements concealed from the public and, even more importantly, from the gaze of prying newspaper editors, for by the late 1640s a number of London's weekly newspapers were running regular exposés of MPs' financial skulduggery. Like their modern-day successors, the newspaper editors had their whistle-blowers to provide them with detailed information about MPs who were allegedly on the make and the amounts of public funds that were finding their way into their pockets.

One of the shrillest and best informed of these whistle-blowers was Clement Walker, a former Exchequer official, who made a second career out of providing newspaper editors with inside information on members' financial peccadilloes. But Walker's most damaging accusation was not that one or another MP had erred, but that the *whole* Westminster system encouraged all parties to use the allowance system and other financial perks to their collective advantage.

The Commons, claimed Walker, was a place where the 'grandees of each party in private close together for their own advancement, serving one another's turn'. Indeed, party rivalries would usually be put aside in order to maintain the lucrative status quo – 'unless something of particular spleen or competition come between them' that caused a temporary breach in this mutually advantageous consensus.

The Commons committee system was a particular target for journalistic attack. 'No committee was so soon made', wrote one disenchanted MP, 'as it was immediately converted to serve the revenge, envy, avarice, or the corrupt humours and passions of the authors'.[6] The main purpose of their dealings, it was claimed, was simply 'to give members advantages of working their own or their friends' business'. And the secretive dealings of the committee system provided the ideal cover whereby financial benefits – whether as allowances, reimbursements, or the provision of grace-and-favour housing – could be conferred with little, if any, public scrutiny. These arrangements, in turn, provided the party leaders with one of the principal foundations of their power; for, as one MP observed, 'he that commands the money commands the men'.

Not that the Commons was wholly deaf to this chorus of public indignation. Periodically, members took steps to placate their critics. More often than not, these corrective measures took the form of yet another committee, charged with vetting members' receipts and accounts, and judging whether public funds had been properly disbursed. And there the accusations tended to disappear, lost in the longest of parliamentary grass.

To some, these gestures at self-regulation were merely play-acting, 'a mere pageant to flourish among the people, for … 'tis madness to imagine the parliament intends to give any account'. Even viewed from inside the Commons, the Houses' attempts to provide a measure of accountability incited little confidence – with one MP dismissing them as merely 'dilusory'.

The inevitable result of these revelations – again in a way that bears extremely clear comparison with recent experience – was a precipitous drop in the standing and public esteem of MPs. Members of the Commons found themselves vilified as 'locusts, caterpillars, and horse-leeches' – or in the pungent phrase of the whistle-blowing Clement Walker, as an 'excoriating rabble of pestiferous vermin'.

Salaries begin

During the reign of Queen Victoria, however, corruption greatly diminished, and by the end of her reign, during which, it may be noted, the Second and Third Reform Acts to extend the voting franchise took place, many of Victoria's more advanced politicians were making the case for a parliamentary salary, so that the House should be open to talent, not just wealth.

An annual salary of £400 was finally introduced in 1911. Lloyd George, as Chancellor of the Exchequer, made the case for it thus:

> When we offer £400 a year as payment of members of parliament it is not recognition of the magnitude of the service, it is not remuneration, it is not a recompense, it is not even a salary. It is just an allowance, and I think the minimum allowance, to enable men to come here, men who would render incalculable service to the State, and whom it is an incalculable loss to the State not to have here, but who cannot be here because their means do not allow it. It is purely an allowance to enable us to open the door to great and honourable public service to these men, for whom this country will be all the richer, all the greater, and all the stronger for the unknown vicissitudes which it has to face by having there to aid us by their counsel, by their courage, and by their resource.[7]

There things largely remained for the rest of the twentieth century, with a few minor adjustments up or down voted on by MPs, until Mr Heath came to power. It was then that things began to go very badly wrong.

1971: allowances begin

At the end of 1970, Willie Whitelaw, then Leader of the House of Commons, told MPs that although they would remain in ultimate control of how much (or how little) they were paid, how much they *should* be paid would be referred to the Top Salaries Review Board (chaired by Lord Boyle). Accordingly, in 1971 the TSRB's report formed the justification for the most fundamental change since the modern salary was introduced to how MPs were paid, and what other benefits and allowances they would receive.[8] At the time, most attention was given to what this would mean for how much MPs would actually be paid *as salary*.

For our purposes, however, we need to pay close attention to what *Boyle* recommended about allowances and expenses, and in particular, what was recommended as any possible subsidised accommodation for MPs alternating between Westminster and their constituencies. To deal with actual pay first: *Boyle*, while instrumental in beginning the process through which MPs would vastly increase their income on the basis of that meaningless, buck-passing 1970s staple, 'comparables', was also the first of many instances when a government would decline the specific salary figure offered to the House.

More importantly, in an ominous and crucial development, *Boyle* concluded that MPs were analogous to civil servants, and recommended some assistance for accommodation purposes.

> This scheme [for MPs] is based on the practice currently in operation for members of the public services who are sent away from their main place of work. Briefly, an allowance based on a fixed daily scale would be paid to cover the reasonable additional cost to provincial members of staying either in London or their constituency, *when engaged on parliamentary duties*. Provincial [i.e. non-London] members would be regarded as living and working either in London or their constituency according to their choice, and would receive the subsistence allowance for the additional cost incurred in attending at their other place of work.[9]

A small first step

As this was in effect the beginning of the great scandal recently revealed, it is crucial that we understand what the first small step was, and so begin to chart accurately the road to the present situation. In the early 1970s MPs demanded, in this particular case at any rate, to be treated like 'other' public sector workers who moved between two sites in the course of their average working week or month.

Within twenty years, this 'right' (an overnight subsistence allowance) was stealthily expanded into something absolutely unimaginable for other workers, private or public, who similarly found themselves 'working' in two places. This was the right to have your family with you, and, on top of that, to make two homes for them. We shall return to what actually constitutes 'work' for an MP, but this was the moment that the system started to go so terribly wrong.

What was to happen in the next two decades was not inevitable. Indeed, Whitelaw formally rejected some of the key details of *Boyle* as they pertained to overnight allowances. But the principle that, by one means or another, MPs' accommodation in two different places should be a taxpayer-funded obligation had been introduced into the system.

Because of what would eventually happen, I need to stress what did not happen in 1971. When the new allowances regime was introduced, post-*Boyle*, it was never expected to provide for a residence, let alone a *home*, any more than the overnight subsistence allowance for civil servants was meant to provide them with a private asset at public expense. Now that the scandal of 2009 has the political class saying, as one, that it should in future be out of the question that MPs be provided with publicly financed *second* homes, we should understand that the system they exploited was never intended to do any such thing.

Apart from anything else, this should serve as a grave warning against installing anything other than the mostly tightly-defined system of allowances. The overnight subsistence allowance was the thin end of the wedge. In 1985 it was officially conceded by the then leader of the House of Commons, John Biffen, in answer to a written question from his Conservative colleague, Tim Eggar, that there was no reason in principle, or in specified fact, why mortgage interest payments rather than hotel bills could not be put forward as a claim. With this achieved, the amount of such allowances exploded.

We should, though, return to the debate in the Commons in late December 1971 on the Ministerial and Other Salaries Bill. For again, we see in embryo the errors of well-meaning politicians, and how a small minority of MPs displayed considerable prescience about what could easily happen were the Bill to become law. Willie Whitelaw assured the House that it would remain sovereign and accountable to the voters for their own actions:

> Provision is also made in the Bill to enable future changes in the salaries which are covered by this Measure to be affected by Order in Council. This change implies a more convenient arrangement. Since the Order in Council will be subject to the affirmative Resolution procedure,

the opportunity for this House to discuss the salary matters will not be prejudiced by this move away from primary legislation.[10]

The going rate...

The reason why I believe MPs have to have a say on their pay is precisely so that the public can have a say on their pay. Whitelaw knew this, and meant it, which is why he promised that it would continue to be the case. But if *Kelly* is implemented, this affirmation that MPs would remain accountable to their electors for their salaries will be set aside. We must anticipate future problems. Once parliament started meekly asking the TSRB, then the Senior Salaries Review Body, to *advise* it on what it should pay itself, *Kelly's* proposal – an external paymaster for MPs, in the form of the Independent Parliamentary Standards Authority – was likely to be only a few steps away.

Whitelaw's intention on allowances

When Whitelaw turned to the overnight allowance, the following, very telling, exchange took place with a sceptical Tory backbencher:

> Mrs Jill Knight (Birmingham, Edgbaston): Am I right in my understanding that those hon. members who do not wish to avail themselves of this money need not take it?

> (Mr Whitelaw): That is the position with all the proposals I am putting forward. It is a perfectly proper arrangement. There have been right hon. and hon. members who have decided in the past not to take their salaries. This has always been recognised as being a wholly private matter between themselves and the Fees Office.

Considerably more scepticism was about to come the way of the Leader of the House. I make no apology for quoting Enoch Powell's speech at length, as, although the results of his prophecies have fortunately been mixed, he was an excellent prophet on the results of the 1971 bill:

> My evidence [to *Boyle*] was against any increase in remuneration or any increase in allowances of any kind and to the effect that the facilities available to members were already larger than conduced to the best possible discharge of their duties...These Motions will contribute to bring about a marked alteration in the status of hon. members of this House. I have deliberately chosen the expression 'contribute to bring about', for when there is a trend or tendency it is rarely possible to point to any one event and say, 'That event, that decision, was decisive; everything after it was different from everything that came before'.

Nevertheless, I believe the alteration in status of members of parliament which is going on, an alteration of which the tendency is to turn them into paid, salaried and pensioned employees, is carried a large and perhaps decisive step further by the Motions before the House...

The more expenses and the more – I was about to say 'generously', but I recoiled from the word; nor will I say 'lavishly' – the more 'largely' expenses are reimbursed, the less will an hon. Member be a person exercising his status at his own discretion and on his own responsibility.

The effect of these Motions goes further...They designate our status not merely as that of employees but as that of full-time employees, employees to be remunerated as full-time employees on a scale which is to be comparable in financial attractiveness to that offered to those in the other professions – or perhaps we should say 'in the professions'...

It is for all of us to put our own interpretation on the status of hon. members and what is conducive to it and what is or could be damaging to it. My case is, not that this is a matter 100 per cent in one direction and 0 per cent in the other, but that there is a dangerous point of balance, a balance which, in my view, we are tipping in the wrong direction by these Motions...not only is our position to be regarded as that of fully remunerated employees on a full-time basis; it is to be pensionable as well. In other words, it is to be a permanent job, a job for life, with a pension beyond it; and provision is to be made, in the event of its untimely termination, as in other forms of employment, for redundancy...

All these provisions together, in my view, add up to a very big step towards a fundamental alteration in the status of a member of parliament. It is, of course, a cumulative change; and with cumulative changes it is particularly difficult to argue, 'Here lies the point at which we pass from one zone to another'; but these are changes so large, and are being made in such a manner, that I believe the occasion is marked as one of danger to the future of this House...

Now of course, we all in this House – and it is of the essence, and has been through the centuries, of parliamentary life – live with the corruption of office: the rewards and the punishments, the disciplines and sanctions which the aspiration to office and to honours – though without it this House and our position in it would be meaningless – nevertheless bring with them.

But we are now in danger, by this change in our status which we are working out, of creating another form of public and open corruption. Every hon. Member knows that we are not only sent here by those who vote, who cast more votes for us than for any of the other candidates at an election. That, of course, is indispensable to our being here; but every hon. Member knows that there are other things which are equally indispensable.

The change which will come about as a result of this alteration in our status – because of our becoming increasingly assimilated to full-time, pensioned employees – is that those who have the voice to say whether we shall or shall not be candidates of our party at a General Election gain a great accession of power over the individual and, thereby, indirectly, over this House.

The Additional Costs allowance

The one area where the government, and the Commons, departed from *Boyle* to any significant degree was in its recommendation that the overnight allowance should be provided by means of a fixed daily rate of subsistence. Whitelaw proclaimed that such a system would be, 'unduly complex, extremely difficult and unsatisfactory to operate and, in some cases, too restrictive'. The government therefore decided upon

> An alternative scheme which would secure the maximum degree of simplicity in its practical application. We have devised a scheme which is based, like the arrangements for the secretarial allowances, which have worked tolerably well, on the reimbursement within an annual limit of hon. members' additional living costs.

Thus a cap was set on how much MPs could spend in the course of a session as their overnight allowance. Not even Powell could possibly have conceived that what was being set in train was the process by which parliament would soon be providing MPs with private homes at public expense.

The big money

I have spent a lot of time on the business of how MPs enabled us to help pay for their homes, because this is by far the most harmful element of the expenses scandal. Jacqui Smith's 88p bath plug or Mark Francois's Pot Noodles are trivia. What corrupted British politics was that our MPs contrived to establish a system under which so many of them were able to provide themselves at public expense with the largest private asset most of us will ever own. That MPs were able, with taxpayers' money, to buy and sell several houses, is almost incredible.

I should perhaps add that I have nothing against anyone who is fortunate enough to live in a nice house in the country. I do myself. But I cannot for the life of me see why, were I an MP, you should have to help finance that. It puzzles me that so many others disagreed.

Much of Chapter 3 will examine what MPs should be paid and why, while Chapter 2 will consider the 2009 expenses scandal itself, and what it tells us about the parties that presided over it. It may be helpful to set out here just what the salary, expenses and allowances regime introduced by Mr Heath's government had come to by 1st April 2009:

Salary: £64,766

Allowances (maximum annual claim)
Staffing expenditure: £103,812
Administrative and Office Expenditure: £22,393
Personal Additional Accommodation Expenditure: £24,222
London Costs Allowance: £7,500
Communications expenditure: £10,400
Motor mileage: 40p per mile (for first 10,000 miles); 25p per mile thereafter

The allowances were also, by decision of parliament, tax-free.

In Chapter 3 I shall come on to the extraordinary subject of MPs' pensions, but for now, here are, supplied by the Office of National Statistics (ONS), figures for average incomes in the United Kingdom in 2008:

Mean gross income: £26,020
Median gross income: £20,801
Top 25%: £31,759
Top 10%: £44,881
Top 5%: £58,917
Top 1%: £118,027

So an MP's salary places him or her in the top 5% income bracket even before the pensions or allowances which provided them with private assets, or special tax exemptions, are taken into account. This is especially relevant when one considers the argument that the allowances have been quietly built into the system only as a compensatory nod and wink to the political sensitivity of index-based salary increases. The majority of MPs who abused the system (measured only by those who have complied with the ad hoc, voluntary repayment scheme) currently plan to stand for re-election. How can the politicians we are about to encounter in the next chapter earn our trust again?

2.
Just greed

After the expenses scandal broke, the Committee on Standards in Public Life held a series of public hearings and invited written submissions from anyone who felt they could suggest how the reputation of parliament could be restored.

One witness was especially caustic. Peter Oborne, in his journalism and books (especially *The Triumph of the Political Class*, 2007, a wonderful book) had long been one of the voices outside Westminster warning politicians what they were doing to themselves, and to us. In typically pungent form, Mr Oborne told the committee that in his opinion the Commons had sunk to a level not seen since Walpole's day.

An earlier witness, the Labour MP Emily Thornberry, explained that her work included the receipt of '1000 submissions a month' from the public, and that that, in large part, justified much of the greatly increased cost of a contemporary parliamentarian. Mr Oborne wondered whether he could have a good look at those pressing communications. If he had been allowed to review what it is that MPs currently do, and consider whether they should do them, we would at least have had a rational basis for beginning to consider what MPs really need in order to carry out their duties. But that was not how *Kelly* proceeded.

Let me quote Peter Oborne's evidence on what much of the political class seems to think it is there for:

> [You've got] a cross-party cabal of theoretically rival whips' offices conspiring together in order to find ways of deceiving the public by secretly rewarding MPs... We have a new political class which has no experience of the rest of the world, or very little, limited experience of it, and so it uses its political role to make a profit... When New Labour came in, [MPs] were sent back to their constituents and were told, 'We do not want you in the House of Commons, go back and be a local MP', and I think that is very, very dangerous. The role of parliament is to scrutinise the actions of the executive ... I think that part of the reason

for the expenses scandal is that successive generations of government whips have basically done a deal with MPs, 'Do not carry out your real role which is to scrutinise legislation and to challenge Ministers, and we will just sort of find money through the back door for you to be paid'. Parliament is a national thing, not a local thing.[1]

Is there something familiar about this? Does it put you in mind of the words of the seventeenth century journalist Clement Walker quoted in Chapter 1?

Perhaps Oborne put it a bit strongly, but MPs were apt to be told that there was an opportunity for them to 'get on the ladder' with the implication 'but not if you are going to be a nuisance'. I believe, however, that even if what seems to be the view of MPs like Ms Thornberry – that an MP today amounts to little more than an ombudsman for failing state services, who might also occasionally hold ministerial office at the pleasure of her party leader – is right, it still cannot justify the cost of modern politicians. But this conception of an MP's role is in fact, in my opinion, wrong, as Peter Oborne says. Sadly the party leaders are all too happy for their MPs to be social workers and duplicates of their local councillors rather than independent-minded private members.

Some of the offenders

Let us look at the very first and perhaps the very worst offenders discovered in this parliament – Derek Conway and Elliot Morley.

Mr Conway was investigated, and the police concluded that the state of parliamentary records was so bad that no useful purpose would be served by taking the matter any further! Mr Conway's conduct was revealed by *The Sunday Times* in 2007 and officially confirmed by the Commons in early 2008. He employed two of his sons at a cost of more than £40,000 to the taxpayer for little evident work.

When this came out, I happened on the morning after to be on the Today programme for an unconnected reason. I was, however, asked whether I thought he should lose the whip. I said that I thought that he should, if the allegations were correct. It was not until several hours later that David Cameron removed it. In any case, should Conway not have been expelled from parliament? His first instinct was to lash out at the Labour party and claim that the stories swirling round him had been made up by their propaganda arm in order to deflect attention from the 'cash for peerages' saga involving Lord Levy.

Later, Conway paid back nearly £17,000, and apologised to the House. He was suspended from the Commons without pay for 10 days and, several months after his actions were revealed, lost the Conservative whip, thus preventing him from being a Tory candidate for the next general election. He still sits in the Commons, he still draws his salary and all his other entitlements, and he will do so while this parliament lasts. He will then, because he is still an MP, receive a considerable 'winding up grant' unless it is forfeited (as in the recent case of Harry Cohen) and a parliamentary pension. I shall return to these pieces of good fortune for Mr Conway, and so many other MPs, shortly.

Then there is Elliot Morley. The former environment minister was investigated by John Lyon, the Parliamentary Standards Commissioner, to see whether his conduct breached the rules of the House. However, Keir Starmer, the Director of Public Prosecutions, has decided that Mr Morley will be charged under the Theft Act over his mortgage claims. His Labour colleagues, Jim Devine and David Chaytor, will also face criminal charges. Upon being charged, all three MPs issued a statement claiming they would attempt to evade the charges through parliamentary privilege.

As I show how the abuses were made possible, I shall keep coming back to specific claims made. One thing, however, is very much worthy of note: though the power exists to do so, not one MP has been expelled from the Commons for his or her conduct. All who wish to continue in place will sit unchallenged until the general election. Surely parliament should expel them?

The main abuses
The Daily Telegraph[2] identified some key abuses from the information it revealed. While they by no means cover them all I shall note them briefly, because whatever other examples I mention, these will become familiar problems.

Flipping, the 'property ladder' & council taxes
Flipping was the practice by which an MP designated a property as the essential 'second home' for the purposes of the allowances regime, claimed for its refurbishment, sold it, and then proceeded to do the same with another property. The 'property ladder' was the expression covering flipping, acquiring, improving and selling property, backed by the public purse, for private gain. The council tax element involved MPs getting that tax paid by the taxpayer for the second home (designated as such to the Commons authorities) while their other home was declared by them to the relevant local council as being a second home. All of this was possible because of a systemic failure in the allowances and expenses regime. I shall explain below the loopholes which demonstrate an indulgence of MPs by officials employed by them. When there is no one guarding the guards, corruption can easily follow.

Last minute repairs & binge-eating

As April and the end of the financial year approached, MPs who had not claimed the full amount available to them frequently bought high value, last-minute items, in order to extract every penny they could from the allowances regime, because – in one of the rare instances of basic financial discipline under the unreformed system – unspent allowances were not rolled over into a new session. Sometimes, when an MP was already due to stand down before the revelations of 2009, properties to be disposed of were refurbished at public expense, and thus put in good order for the estate agents' brochures.

Binge-eating was the newspaper's term for the practice of claiming the full £400, entirely unverified, food allowance, month in, month out (£4800 a year) regardless of actual expenditure. All three of these flaws involve the same thing: the untrammelled willingness of so many MPs to milk the system.

'Long distance shoppers' & 'maxing out'

MPs used their allowances to buy valuable household goods, theoretically for their second homes, but which then arrived wherever the MP actually lived. Meanwhile, until very recently, most claims for items under £250 required no receipts. So there was a plethora of claims for goods priced at £249. Both these defects were aspects of a system intended to make it difficult to check the facts.

Capital gains tax & the wrong address

CGT is an area where MPs have, in my opinion, been unfairly attacked. Inland Revenue guidelines make it clear that where a person has two homes i.e. places where he spends quite a bit of time, he is quite at liberty to choose which one of them is the one on which he will be free of capital gains tax. He does not have to show that it is in any sense his principal residence. Some MPs may have designated a place which could not properly be described as a home, and that is of course wrong. Where, however, an MP has two houses, both of which he uses quite a bit, he is not required, just as no one else is required, to choose the one in which he spends most time.

I believe that MPs should never have been able to claim greater expenses in respect of second homes than the cost of staying in hotels, but that does not affect the fact that it has been unfair, as I see it, to accuse them of avoiding capital gains tax by choosing between two genuine homes.

Some Conservative MPs

I now move on to a sample of backbench Conservative MPs: Anthony Steen, Sir Peter Viggers and Bill Wiggin. The first two are standing down at the next election. Anthony Steen got into difficulties because he claimed £87,000 for a constituency home which, he rather incautiously told a radio journalist, 'some people think looks rather like Balmoral'. But as Mr Steen's housing claim was considerably lower than, for example, that of his party leader, what really lost him his future parliamentary career was that pithy phrase about Balmoral. In the immediate aftermath, the Conservative party's media operation (led by Andy Coulson) reacted with fury to the fact that Mr Steen's remarks caused the 'media narrative' to return to being stories of 'rich Tories' living unapologetically in large houses. A telephone call from Mr Cameron to Mr Steen followed, and having until then vehemently insisted that he would stand again, Mr Steen bowed to pressure from his leader and announced that he would no longer contest the next election.

Why was Mr Cameron's telephone call so persuasive? Because Anthony Steen had learnt the same lesson as all other MPs from the fate of Howard Flight during the 2005 general election. Thanks to powers granted to them by this Labour government, local candidates are nominated by their party leaders, rather than their local constituency associations. So, as Mr Howard forcefully pointed out to Howard Flight, they can also decline to nominate them. This undemocratic centralisation of power in the hands of party leaders is one of the key things which need to be changed if parliament is to be properly reformed.

Sir Peter Viggers, meanwhile, has become almost emblematic of the great scandal, for he was the MP who claimed and indeed, alerted a great many of us to the very existence of, a £1,645 floating 'duck island'. Yet although Sir Peter did receive an impressive £20,000 for gardening expenses in general, his overall expenses were no higher than average. The problem was the words 'duck island'. He did not actually receive public funds for his ducks! The duck island was that rare thing: a claim that was declined. With much less resistance than others who fell under the spotlight, Sir Peter gracefully slipped away and announced, more or less of his own free will, that he would not contest his seat at the next election.

On the same day that Sir Peter made his first appearance in The Daily Telegraph, the paper also turned its attention to Bill Wiggin. A school contemporary of his leader, Mr Wiggin had claimed £11,000 in mortgage expenses on a house that did not have a mortgage. Mr Cameron accepted that this was completely inadvertent. The former merchant banker (UBS, Kleinwort Benson and Commerzbank) had, on 23 different forms, filed the wrong address for his claim, until the mistake was realised, but not revealed, in 2006. After news of this broke last year, Mr Wiggin followed Mr Cameron's call for MPs affected by the *Telegraph's* stories to 'meet the public' to explain themselves. Mr Wiggin's meeting, though billed as open to all his electors who could attend, was filmed with the door open to those 'invited by Bill' but closed to those who were not. At the time Mr Wiggin was a junior spokesman. He has since been promoted to a senior whip and will be contesting his seat.

The Conservative scrutiny panel

I shall return to Sir Thomas and Sir Paul, but first I want to deal with what was one of the most praised aspects of Mr Cameron's response to the crisis. This was the internal Conservative 'scrutiny panel', comprising two whips, a party officer, a lawyer and two Conservative officials (including Mr Cameron's chief of staff). Its work produced some £125,000 of 'voluntary' repayments, but it missed many problems entirely, as it did many others. If you were feeling well disposed towards the parties, you could call this an effort hampered by amateurism. If you are not, it is hard to see the Conservative scrutiny panel as anything other than a gimmick.

All three men still sit as MPs in receipt of the Conservative whip.

Housing

While far from being the only allowance abused systematically by MPs, the one that has caused the most headlines has been the ACA – the Additional Costs Allowance (now called the Personal Additional Accommodation Expenditure, or PAAE). This, extended vastly beyond its original purposes, was what gave MPs their gardeners, their second homes and all the luxuries inside. In 1985 MPs were told by the then Leader of the House that 'there is no reason why [they] should not claim mortgage interest payments against this allowance'.

In 1994, 'when centralised civil service subsistence rates no longer applied', the House increased its rate again. In 2001 the Senior Salaries Review Board declined to recommend what the ACA should be. The Commons, however, agreed to a backbench amendment significantly raising it. The crucial point is that the maximum permitted ACA in fact went from £187.50 in 1972 to £23,083 in 2007/08.

In the last decade alone, parliaments with huge Labour majorities ensured that the ACA increased substantially more than the RPI. But during its first decade of operation, those involved explicitly, but futilely, tried to keep it in line with other, similar civil service allowances – such as the 'regular visitor' rate for public sector workers who had to spend time in London. The MPs' allowance was originally intended simply as an overnight subsistence payment for MPs who wished to be treated like 'other' civil servants. Yet nowhere else in the public sector did such expenses move from including hotel bills to rent, then to mortgage payments, then to food, utilities and council tax. Even cleaning, insurance payments, telephone and satellite television bills all somehow joined the list, which was eventually to culminate in the duck island fiasco.

With every penny that MPs claimed, they did so having solemnly declared every year, 'I incurred these costs wholly, exclusively and necessarily to enable me to stay overnight away from my only or main home for the purpose of performing my duties as a Member of parliament'.

Question Time fracas

After the expenses dam broke there was broadcast a wild edition of the BBC's *Question Time*. All the politicians on the panel were booed loudly, while Kevin Easterbrook, CEO of the fast food chain McDonalds, was cheered to the rafters. His most popular point was the traditional business adage that one should not make a profit out of one's expenses, which is truer still of the civil service. How incomprehensible it still seems that MPs ever came to delude themselves that different rules applied to them.

Sheer greed has led to the present disastrous situation. Luckily the Freedom of Information (FoI) legislation has made it possible to find out what politicians had been up to all these years. By overwhelming majorities, a bipartisan effort was made by the political class to try to prevent their subjection to the FoI scrutiny they had imposed on the rest of the country. We should not forget that, but for the *Telegraph's* intervention, this effort would have very largely succeeded without complaint from either main party. As I shall show, the postures struck by both the Labour and Tory leaderships, when they thought anything like full disclosure could still be prevented, were in their own way as telling as anything the expenses mole revealed.

Alistair Darling's claims

Taxes are not enjoyable, but we all have to pay them, except perhaps some of the more outré parliamentary candidates and members of the House of Lords and, of course, on a substantial amount of their turnover, by MPs. Even the Chancellor of the Exchequer himself took what he could from his friends in Her Majesty's Revenue & Customs. Through his expenses claims the public bought Alistair Darling a £265 vacuum cleaner. I have to admit surprise here, that it was even possible to pay so much for a vacuum cleaner! Was it manufactured by Bentley? Buying top rate vacuum cleaners with the public purse is one thing, but government ministers creating laws that apply to us but not to them is quite another.

Mr Darling switched the designation of his second home between London and his Edinburgh constituency *four times*, allowing him to claim £2,500 in stamp duty and legal fees when he bought his London flat, and more than £4,000 to furnish it. Leaving to one side the benefits he got from his allowances, it was the fact that he was able to avoid a tax he imposes on the rest of us as hated as Stamp Duty that irked.

Alistair Darling further charged £763.75 to the public for an accountant to prepare his self-assessment form for him – an onerous regime Labour itself had introduced.[3] So the very form he had introduced himself was so difficult to complete that he had to employ an accountant to do it! Eight other members of the cabinet did the same thing. Indeed, Dennis Bates, the husband of Meg Munn, MP, got £5,000 altogether, from the taxpayer, for providing tax advice to MPs, including the Foreign Secretary David Miliband and his own wife. Given that accountancy fees incurred in complying with the law are not allowable against tax, the results of the investigation HMRC is currently conducting into MPs who did this will be interesting – if, of course, we get to hear about it!

Something must have been in the air at the Treasury, for one of Mr Darling's junior ministers was Kitty Ussher, who claimed a generous £20,000 for repairs to her London home. What appears to have caused her to resign as Exchequer Secretary was the allegation that she had flipped the designation of one her homes before she sold it in order to avoid over £10,000 worth of Capital Gains Tax. As I have explained earlier I do not think there is anything wrong at all in choosing which of two homes, provided they are homes upon which you pay capital gains tax. Why Kitty Ussher fell while others escaped is hard to explain. Whatever the source of her bad luck, Miss Ussher subsequently decided to stand down at the next election. Both she and Mr Darling retain the Labour whip, and he, of course, intends to stand again.

Parliament's attempts at concealment

We know what we do because the *Telegraph's* mole provided them with the intelligence they used to such devastating effect. But the material leaked was only compiled in the first place because MPs across the House had, at public expense naturally, fought and lost a series of extremely expensive legal actions to try to prevent the effects of FoI legislation applying to them.

The first rebuffed FoI request came from Heather Brooke, an Anglo-American journalist who had had some experience of using US FoI legislation at a state level to investigate the routine expenses of politicians. When Heather Brooke started making

FoI requests, she expected little more than mundane and trivial, but occasionally piquantly newsworthy, items to be the fruit of her efforts. However, as parliament fought to keep just about everything secret, others joined Brooke in making requests. A joint appeal in 2005 to the Information Commissioner, Jon Ungoed-Thomas, and the response of the Commons, led by Speaker Michael Martin, led to a four year legal battle which, I am pleased to say, the MPs eventually lost. Their partial concession to legal defeat was to prepare to release heavily edited versions of their expenses claims, but it was the uncensored information that was so famously leaked.

Squalid, bipartisan collusion

Even this very partial disclosure of the facts, however, would not have been prepared if one of the key members of the Tory establishment had got his way in 2007. David Maclean, MP, chief whip under three successive leaders, introduced, with the connivance of his own front bench and of government whips, a private member's bill to exempt parliament from the provisions of the Freedom of Information Act. Despite being the sole MP to speak in favour of his bill, the Commons passed it by 96 votes to 25.

It is remarkable that these hundred enemies of FoI were to be found in Westminster on a Friday afternoon – a time long since given over by the vast majority of MPs to constituency business. Particularly disgracefully, the presiding deputy speakers (Tory Sir Michael Lord and Labour Sylvia Heal) allowed closure votes, which prevented opponents of the bill from using parliamentary procedure to talk it out, and despite the fact that little over a sixth of the Commons was present for the vote. No such closure motions had been allowed by the chair for over twenty years! When it got to the House of Lords, however, no sponsor could be found for it, and their Lordships' Select Committee on the Constitution attacked it lustily. Well done, their Lordships! When, shortly afterwards, Gordon Brown became Prime Minister, his official spokesman indicated that the Maclean bill no longer stood any chance of getting government time to make any more progress through parliament and so it died.

All these expedients to prevent FoI taking its toll having failed, the courts ruled in May 2008 that 'the expenditure of public money through the payment of MPs' salaries and allowances is a matter of direct and reasonable interest to taxpayers', and so I return again to where all that public money went.

Alan Duncan

When the millionaire former oil trader Alan Duncan made his claims, he fell some distance short of claiming the maximum allowable figure. However, one expense he did insist upon claiming for, despite being warned by the Fees office that it might seem 'excessive', was a £4,000 gardening bill that included the purchase of a ride-on lawnmower. It was a decision both he and his leader surely came to regret, since Mr Duncan was shadow leader of the house, and therefore Mr Cameron's official spokesman on parliamentary allowances, when the *Telegraph's* revelations were unleashed.

Mr Duncan persisted an awfully long time as Mr Cameron's chief parliamentary adviser on expenses. The Tory leader was eventually obliged to drop him after a series of indiscretions threatened to bury them both. The year before, Mr Duncan had appeared on the BBC's *Have I Got News For You* programme, and he was asked by *Private Eye* editor Ian Hislop whether he, an already wealthy man, claimed on his second home. Mr Duncan answered, 'It's a fabulous system, isn't it? It's a great system'. Oddly enough, the programme found these words amusing enough to repeat after the scandal broke. The final straw for David Cameron was, presumably, Mr Duncan being secretly recorded saying that MPs had to live on 'rations'. Soon after this he was demoted from the shadow cabinet to a more junior position. I must say, however, that Alan Duncan made no attempt at all, as far as I know, to conceal anything.

It is natural to have sympathy with him for being exploited by someone to whom he had offered hospitality in an effort to state his case. What is not possible is to accept a system that needlessly gave quite so much public money away. Mr Duncan remains in receipt of the Tory whip, is on the front bench and intends to stand again.

Cameron's transparent claims

While David Maclean and Michael Martin were trying to 'solve' the problem of MPs' expenses from one angle, some, inside and outside the Commons, did sincerely try to reform the system before the storm broke. Others claimed they already had. In July 2008, David Cameron announced 'transparency reforms', declaring that (almost) all Conservative MPs' staff, employed family members, were now publishing the office running costs, and travel and accommodation expenditure incurred by MPs outside of London. This was an exaggeration, but Mr Cameron continued:

> Politicians need to do everything they can to regain the trust of the British people, and transparency has a key part to play in that process. We must show that we're spending taxpayers' money sensibly and correctly. We are the first party to demand this information from our members, and our MPs are voluntarily revealing a much more detailed

breakdown of their expenses than official rules require them to. I'm glad that we're leading the way.

Though such premature optimism and self-congratulation was challenged by a few brave MPs and others, both front benches conspired to keep information from the public at every turn. When the scandal of MPs employing family members was personified by the Conway affair, what was the response of the House to the obvious worry that many other MPs might be employing their relatives, perhaps at higher than average parliamentary salaries and sometimes to do very little indeed? A full inquiry of suspected past abuse? A vigorous determination to at least show who was employing whom on the basis of what direct, personal relationship? Not at all. What the Commons in fact did was to grant itself a lengthy grace period in which MPs could get embarrassing relatives or partners off the public payroll, or at least shifted over to other MPs. Only once this was safely achieved were such relationships that remained to be registered and declared. This parliament, whatever else it has done, has never lost its consistency.

MPs refuse to save themselves

In June 2008 the Members Estimates Committee (MEC) published a long-heralded report on allowances, provoked in part by the secrets which had already seeped out. It was perhaps too generous to itself in saying of its own findings that they amounted to a 'root and branch review' designed to 'meet public expectations for clearer audit and transparency'. Even so, they were too much for the House of Commons, which promptly voted the vast bulk of its recommendations down. Likewise, 2008's Baker report – Sir John Baker was the retiring chairman of the SSRB – was largely dismissed, and entirely so where it threatened to reduce allowances or salary. The pattern was monotonous: when warning bells sounded, MPs ignored them; when fires broke out, they were left to burn themselves out.

In the red corner

Even distinguished socialist dynasties have become involved. Husband and wife MPs Alan and Ann Keen – the latter the sister of Sylvia Heal, the Deputy Speaker – used each of their separate second homes allowances to buy one central London apartment whose mortgage has so far cost the public £175,128. Both Mr and Mrs Keen have outer London seats roughly a half hour cab journey from Westminster.

Both MPs still receive their party's whip and intend to stand again.

When I list MPs affected by the expenses crisis, citing any particular individual is to engage in a perhaps random selection of revelations produced by the press thus far. Why did he resign? Why did she stay? Is that worse than this? On issue after issue one can try holding different MPs up against one another, but all this accomplishes is a rather superficial ranking of their guilt. But there are some insights. For example, those MPs whose stories were revealed first, en masse, benefited from a 'bunching effect', the impact of individual stories being lost. MPs whose expenses were detailed later, often in isolation, have been much more likely to suffer political penalties. Once the leadership of each of the three main parties felt confident that it was staying in place, varying efforts were made to exploit the crisis for factional purposes. As with so much else in this parliament, Mr Cameron has performed far more adroitly than Mr Brown.

Look after your friends

Yet Mr Cameron has not purged his party, merely skimmed it. He has picked off the obviously vulnerable and has barely exercised a fraction of the powers with which he has equipped himself, both effectively to dismiss sitting MPs and to control the selection of new ones. I shall suggest below that the fact that one of his closest colleagues, Michael Gove, was one of those most deeply affected by the revelations, is central to this failure to purge.

Before I turn to that, another peculiarity of the crisis is how well brazenness still pays. It paid literally when claims were being made and the Fees Office's bluff was being called. Those who were scrupulous enough actually (and frequently unnecessarily) to detail what they were claiming for, have in all too many cases simply been ridiculed for their choice of sweet or crisp. Also, if you compare those MPs who have decided, for whatever reason, to stand down, with those at least as compromised who have determined to go on, and you will find no obvious rhyme or reason. Justice has been largely absent in the unwinding of this scandal.

Michael Gove

The late Frank Johnson, once editor of *The Spectator* and doyen of parliamentary sketch writers, said that you could write anything of just about anyone, and they would take it in more or less good part. From Hollywood stars down to the lowliest politicians, prudence alone dictated that they should at least smile, no matter how sharp the barb. The one exception Mr Johnson noted to his own rule was journalists. Were he, at *The Spectator* for instance, to commission a mildly sceptical review of, say, a book by someone as distinguished as Sir Harold Evans, it would find, immediately upon publication, that outraged demands would follow for a right of reply at enormous length, learned friends would be cited, if not actually employed, and raw, personal pain would angrily be expressed.

Michael Gove's part in the parliamentary expenses scandal of 2009 showed how right Frank Johnson was. For of all the MPs contacted by the *Telegraph* during its long list of shame last year, the only parliamentarian to threaten them with legal action, prior even to publication, was Mr Gove.

What had the shadow education secretary done that required such (futile, as it turned out) cost? In just a few short months after his election in 2005, Mr Gove had mastered the allowances regime. A £500 bill for a night in a five-star hotel was a bagatelle compared to the public money spent first on Mr Gove's West London home before he flipped it. He spent £7,000 in five months in London. £13,000 in stamp duty and other fees for these early property moves were also claimed and paid as parliamentary expenses.

Showing the talent that made him such a successful journalist, he managed, as the axe swung ever closer, with the *Telegraph* day by day proceeding through first the government, then promising to reach higher reaches of the opposition, to be the one victim of the scandal to try to perform a classic spoiler on the paper. Friendly journalists retailed Michael Gove's defence the evening before the story hit the streets.

> 'I am aware' [said Mr Gove] 'that many of my constituents commute but to my mind the best thing that I can do is be available when they need me, commit to working as hard as possible for them but also stress the importance of my family life generally. If people don't see their family then sooner or later there will be a crash, a burn out and a heavy price to pay.'

> This struck me at the time [said Fraser Nelson] as being oddly frank: he was saying he tried the commute, couldn't hack it, and told his constituents that for family reasons he was moving his family back to London which would have been his main home and he would spend three days a week in the constituency. Ergo, his second residence would change, from London to Surrey Heath. This isn't a Blears-style property speculation, but a genuine change of circumstances.[4]

But it was not all that frank, as the second home was not in the constituency, nor was the defence overly appealing to many of his constituents, large numbers of whom would find their daily London commute much more comfortable if their arrival in town could be followed by a simple walk across the river from the station to their place of work. But his friends had made their case: flipping was not objectionable when you had a reason.

But there was more to come from Gove and, to Mr Cameron's horror, it threatened to embroil the leader himself in the scandal beyond the matter of his own expenses. For it turned out that Mr Gove's essential requirements for being an MP which included a £331 Chinon armchair, a £493 Manchu cabinet, a pair of elephant lamps for £134.50, and other expensive items, were bought from a shop called OKA, which benefited from many thousands of pounds of purchases, thanks to the taxpayer. It happens to be owned by Mr Cameron's mother-in-law, Lady Astor.

There are questions to be asked about this. What went through the minds of Tory MPs, several of them frontbenchers, who spent thousands of pounds of public money in a private commercial enterprise they knew was owned by a close relative of the man who in effect employed, and certainly promoted them? What did Mr Cameron himself think, for that matter, of the fact that some of his MPs were doing this?

When Mr Gove, in anticipation of the *Telegraph's* revelations, employed no less a lawyer than Anthony Julius to assert that his client had 'complete and compelling' answers to all the paper's questions, what did he hope would happen to the story about to be published?[5] Mr Julius went as far as to say that if it was even hinted that Mr Gove had merely broken the spirit of the rules, his client would of course take 'appropriate steps to defend his reputation'. The actual action Mr Gove ended up taking was volunteering to repay £7,000, saying sorry fulsomely in the press, then holding one of the earlier 'apology meetings' in his constituency.

Like so many others, Mr Gove's apology meeting was an oddly truncated affair, with local newspapers reporting that while association members got in easily enough, the theoretically open meeting was not quite so accessible to other, less well-disposed voters.[6] Although a few did get in, the meeting served its purpose by being well briefed to the national press as having been a success from Mr Gove's point of view. But there was an illuminating detail reported by *The Guardian*. '[When] one angry ex-serviceman told Gove that during a surgery session the politician had talked to him about integrity and asked if he could not go back to work, there was a ripple of embarrassment. 'I have more integrity than you will ever have mate,' the former soldier said. A smattering of applause was hushed by collective tutting.'[7] This must have been an unattractive display of braying loyalty.

No one can doubt Michael Gove's talents. I certainly do not. David Cameron rightly never has, and that is why he asked the freshman MP to play a central role in his successful leadership campaign. It is presumably why, when it emerged that Mr Gove had, for example, tried to lure no less a figure than Lord Levy to the Tory party this was smiled upon indulgently. How then to measure the man's worth? The independent website, They Work For You, records that Michael Gove ranked joint first in both 2007/2008 and 2006/2007 for his ACA claims, spending, respectively, £23,083 and £22,110. Evidently such wit and intelligence has come to the public at a price. For OKA it has returned a handsome profit.

The Speakers

As the expenses scandal unfurled, disrupting all three major parties, a distraction was needed. They came up with the expulsion of Speaker Martin. This was chiefly the doing of the government. Labour had put him in place, and as the wave of public anger rolled over them, it was the Prime Minister himself who dispensed with him. The three leaders offered tributes as he went, but getting rid of the Speaker behind whom all three parties had sheltered as he sought so valiantly, and expensively, to protect them and their MPs from the consequences of their own actions was a cynical act. The speakership election served to distract politicians and some in the press – though fewer, I suspect, of the public – from the real scandal. Its consequence was the election of Speaker Bercow.

True to form, Mr Bercow flipped. His second home designation changed in April-June 2009, just in time to inherit the Speaker's state apartment. This was perfectly legal, but such a telling contrast with his former heroine, Lady Thatcher, who when she became Prime Minister, consistently declined the salary the SSRB recommended for her. Earlier, the Fees Office had been reduced to sending the future Speaker a letter in January 2007 sadly observing that he had not provided a mortgage interest statement for more than two years. CGT of £6,508 was avoided – and then, in the midst of the speakership election, volunteered to HMRC. For four separate years Mr Bercow managed to be one of the joint highest ACA claimants and to round it off, the future Speaker had spent just under a thousand pounds worth of public funds to have an accountant prepare his taxes for him.

As late as July 2009 . . .

In July 2009, early in his speakership and without public fanfare, Mr Bercow presided over a new, interim expenses regime permitting MPs to claim up to £9,125 a year without producing receipts. This measure, pre-empting *Kelly* or anything else, was brought into effect without even·a debate in the House. The speakership is central to the chances of the Commons recovering its former standing. Tradition dictates this and, as we shall see, the proposals of both the Labour government and *Kelly* still acknowledge great importance in the role of the Speaker.

Mr Bercow, a relatively young man, stands to be particularly well rewarded for his services. His pension pot, for example, even if he sits only into his early 60s, will easily exceed £2 million. Material considerations will probably not affect Mr Bercow's speakership. Yet something, even so early in his reign, seems to be troubling him. At the end of 2009 Mr Bercow told *Total Politics* magazine that he saw considerable merit in no longer facing the voters. He suggested giving the Speaker 'a separate constituency, known as St Stephen's, representing a small area around Westminster'. As the whole point would be that ordinary members of the public would not be allowed to be 'constituents' of the Speaker, *represent* is hardly an accurate description.

The fact that the MPs of this parliament have found confidence in this man to be their Speaker gives me no confidence at all that he is the Speaker the country needs. But let me return to what we know about MPs.

Outside earnings

Not everything we know comes from the big leak of 2009. As a result of the various scandals that affected parliament in Sir John Major's time, registers today detail what MPs earn apart from their Commons' salaries. I shall say in the next chapter why I believe it is definitely desirable that MPs should indeed have outside employment. Plenty do. The shadow cabinet, for example, has earned a lot outside parliament. While they prepare for government, its members also earn substantial amounts of additional money. In the wake of the expenses scandal, however, Mr Cameron announced in July 2009 that such earnings should cease, after a six month grace period.

Labour, with a handful of Blairite exceptions, such as Alan Milburn, Stephen Byers and John Reid, have shown much less aptitude for earning private money. But I want to again make the point; I have no objection to those who have done so, either in opposition or as backbenchers. Ministers, on the other hand, should, I believe, be doing a full time job and not earn outside money. Let us look at what some of them have charged the public.

Some ministerial expenses

Scottish Secretary Jim Murphy claimed £594.55 for Christmas cards; the current Home Secretary, Alan Johnson, spent £8,289.04 in 2007 on a machine which folds paper and inserts it into envelopes, filling and sealing as many as 2,200 envelopes an hour, which is always a nice thing for a constituency office, or for that matter, local party or association to have; and the tourism minister Barbara – 'wife', as the papers like to say, 'of multi-millionaire novelist Ken' – Follett rather let London's image down by claiming £25,000 for 'security patrols', apparently needed to enable her to walk the length of the pedestrianised West London street on which her Georgian townhouse was located.

All these ministers are still in place. Phil Hope is not. The former health minister claimed and then, subsequent to discovery, paid back, £41,709 for his designated second home, a 511 sq ft flat in South London. Former cabinet member and Labour party chair Hazel Blears is not there either. Admittedly she resigned before she was sacked, calling on the Prime Minister to quit. She also flipped three times, made the customary declarations to HMRC as regards CGT, and in the interregnum, before denouncing Mr Brown and while trying to hold onto her cabinet place, tearfully held up in front of the cameras a cheque for £13,332 she had decided to volunteer by way of CGT.

Shaun Woodward, former Tory MP, now Labour cabinet member, carries through life, whenever his name appears, the additional tag, 'married to Sainsbury's heiress, Camilla'. As an MP, he claimed more than £100,000 to pay the interest on a multi-million pound London flat, one of at least seven properties he owned, including a 6-storey Queen Anne townhouse in Westminster. In a perfect example of how the sheer scope of the scandal sometimes overwhelmed its coverage, when his expenses were detailed, Mr Woodward did not dispute the six figure sum of public money, but instead quibbled with *The Daily Telegraph* over a Muller crunch yoghurt (38p) and an Asda pizza (£1.06), both of which had, he informed us, been consumed by a member of his staff and not by him. This was taking to extremes a classic tactic of the spin doctors who have done so much to breed cynicism in modern political life, whereby if one can rebut a part of the story, however peripheral, and focus upon that, it distracts attention and detracts credibility from the greater substance.

Shaun Woodward – a long-time BBC employee – bears comparison with his predecessor and successor as MP for Witney. His defection opened up the seat for a Tory candidate, who was not elected in 1997, to get a safe seat for 2001 – David Cameron. Mr Woodward had succeeded Douglas Hurd – a man who during his own leadership bid in 1990 had been unfairly ridiculed for saying nothing other than the truth, which was that instead of being to the manner born, he was the son of a tenant farmer and itinerant journalist. Mr Cameron and Mr Hurd went to the same school, but it is Mr Cameron and Mr Woodward who are surely exemplary members of the modern political class, not Douglas Hurd.

I wonder whether it worries some MPs that there were some highly honourable men and women amongst them? Philip Hollobone, a Tory, claimed just £43,737 in expenses when the average claim was £135,600 (and a neighbouring Labour MP's was £157,646). From the staffing allowance Mr Hollobone restricted himself to £400, while most MPs spent almost all the £90,505 on offer! Self-made multi-millionaire Geoffrey Robinson, a Labour MP, and possibly one of the richest men in the House, set an example to all his wealthy compatriots by not claiming a penny on the ACA. Nor do fellow Labour MPs Celia Barlow and Martin Salter claim for second homes. The same can be said of five Conservatives – Adam Afriyie, Richard Benyon, Philip Dunne, Anne Milton and Rob Wilson. Eight MPs have claimed nothing by way of travel expenses.

Within the rules

During the season of revelations a defence was offered that MPs' behaviour had been 'within the rules'. The appointment first of Sir Thomas Legg to assess the matter retrospectively, then of the retired Judge Sir Paul Kennedy to hear 'appeals' from Sir Thomas' findings, indicated that the three party leaderships did not care to offer this argument. MPs after all are, in real terms, paid more now than they ever have been before.[8] The number of staff they have available to them has exploded. In the first ten years of Labour being in office the number employed went from 1,753 (for 659 MPs) to 2,694 (for 646 MPs). Yet this is in a period when power and responsibility was draining away from Westminster – largely to Brussels of course, but also downwards through devolution – at a rapid and, as far as Brussels is concerned, highly depressing rate. So why do they need, in addition to their pay, enormous allowances?

Government and opposition tried to cope with the scandal. The Prime Minister produced *Kelly* and, with some reluctance, he has agreed to implement essentially all its recommendations, putting most of them into statutory effect by using the Parliamentary Standards Act, 2009. The grave defects in this approach are the main subject of the next chapter. Lacking both the power of office, and the responsibility that comes with it, the leader of the Opposition took advantage of Mr Brown's characteristically ponderous approach. Early on in this crisis, harsh *future* scrutiny was promised and an end to past abuses offered although, as we have seen, condemnation of the abuses was distinctly erratic.

Labour has earned the public's contempt by its behaviour in office over the last decade, which has made so much of this scandal possible, and for its disastrous handling of the economy. In my final chapter I shall therefore pay special attention to what the likely next Conservative government is pledged to do. One particularly discouraging sign was that at his much praised press conference at the St Stephen's Club in the first week of the crisis, and again in his party's formal submission to *Kelly*, the Tory leader still defended the payment of mortgage interest relief to MPs. This reluctance, this need to be dragged by the ears towards honourable behaviour, is as much the mark of Mr Cameron as Mr Brown's shabby routines are of him.

The Prime Minister's answer to the crisis, or more precisely, his effort to hold on to control of his parliamentary party during the dying months of his government, has been to offer backbench MPs a £3,000 pay rise which he proposes to fund out of a commensurate pay cut in ministers' salaries. Neither man sought to solve this crisis before it was revealed. Now that some of the truth stands in front of us, each apparently intends to do as little as he can get away with.

The old class can be pungent enough about the new. Writing just as the stories began to emerge, Norman Tebbit looked back on his parliamentary career and observed:

> The more generous expenses were considered compensation for the fact that the boys didn't think they were getting the sort of pay they expected...But there's a spivery around it now. It's like the benefits culture. It reminds me of the guy who is on disability benefit and goes out window cleaning. I call them welfare junkies and I am afraid that is too close to the truth for some MPs...A lot of people who are very comfortably off were simply milking the system to enlarge their property portfolio. The moats, the tennis courts, weren't necessities. The whole thing should be replaced by a simple daily allowance for staying in London overnight. Why should I as a taxpayer pay for their new flat-screen televisions? They don't need all these lamps and rugs...When I arrived in 1970 almost everyone had done another job...Now they start out as political advisers. There's a political class, they are very inward-looking, they don't understand life. It is more corrupt because they have more in common with each other than with people outside.[9]

This was why Lord Tebbit advised voters during the European elections in 2009 to send the new class a message by not voting for any of the three complicit Westminster parties. For his pains, he was threatened with expulsion by Mr Cameron, but who can honestly say that any of the parties have yet heard what the people are trying to say to them?

3.
The people are the masters

Having refused to reform themselves when they were getting away with it, MPs declined to reform themselves once they were caught. Instead, they handed responsibility for this to Sir Christopher Kelly and the Committee on Standards in Public Life.

Yet *Kelly* declines to say why the crisis occurred. The committee, which prided itself on not being rushed, disclaimed any responsibility for investigating the past. But we cannot have confidence that matters will be put right unless we understand what went wrong and why. As things stand, the mechanism which parliament itself has provided is the Legg inquiry. There have been some confessions by MPs, but these seem to be expected by the guilty, to be followed by absolution as long as the money wrongly taken had been paid back.

We need to find out the truth

This is not good enough. We cannot hope to have a renewed House of Commons if its members have pardoned themselves. In order to restore trust, the first thing we need is a proper investigation. The Crown Prosecution Service must be instructed to look carefully into anything in the Legg enquiry which suggests a breach of the criminal law.

It has been put strongly to me that this should go back further in time than the Legg enquiry has, but although there is certainly a case for that, a line does have to be drawn somewhere and I am inclined to think it has been drawn in the right place.

Courts deal with crimes

The lesson from the past is one which *Kelly* has failed to recognise: the remedy for MPs who break laws must be the law. And laws must be enforced by courts. My greatest disagreement with *Kelly* therefore, and with the regime that the three largest parties all wish to introduce in response to this crisis, is their desire that it should be based on yet another half-way house off-shoot of parliament such as is intended by the Independent Parliamentary Standards Authority (IPSA). Instead of broken laws being dealt with by judges, 'transgressions' will be assessed by an agency still dominated at every turn by the Commons, and whose relationship to the courts is unclear.

We should learn from the past: in the nineteenth century the one thing MPs could not necessarily be trusted to do was to ensure that their own courts were honestly administered, so electoral courts were invented. Election law, passed by parliament, removed from parliament the burden of policing its own elections. In this century we have seen all too plainly that questioning vast allowances and expenses is not in practice going to be done by MPs. It will not be done effectively by something that is established intentionally – precisely because it is *not* a court.

Abolish the IPSA

IPSA has been established by the Parliamentary Standards Act of 2009 (PSA, 2009). This act needs to be substantially amended, if not repealed, but IPSA should be abolished. I will come to IPSA's intended function as paymaster for MPs, but for now I consider its task as regulator, policeman and pseudo-judge.

The problem with giving anything other than a court of law any power over the Commons is that this risks being a breach of parliamentary privilege (literally, 'private law' – see *Kelly*, p109). Parliamentary privilege is the concept, correct in my opinion, that parliament should be sovereign in its own domain. It includes matters such as the absolute freedom of speech of MPs in parliament (guaranteed by Article 9 of the Bill of Rights 1688). The exercise by parliament of control over its own affairs is known as 'exclusive cognisance', and ordinarily, this should be sacrosanct. For it is parliamentary privilege that in so many ways ensures the freedom and independence of parliament. But these are not ordinary circumstances, and they require proper solutions, not fig leaves.

No one supports the rights of parliament, and of its individual members, more than I do. But the crux of the matter is this: we need to move away from the concept of a 'private law' intended to protect MPs. It exists to protect us, and to protect them in order to protect *us*. It cannot be right that it has been stretched to entrench monetary rewards for MPs.

In the past, in the very recent past, being an MP brought with it neither a high salary nor immense benefits. It now does both, and the basis on which those things are enjoyed needs to be put into a modern context. MPs, in receipt of public funds which they have provided for themselves in the form of salaries, pensions and allowances, have to be completely honest and open about them.

We must decide how abuse can be *deterred*: prevention is better than cure. My suggestion is to create a specific court to consider any possible abuses, and to deal with them expertly and swiftly. Call it the 'Court of Parliament', let it be seated in as ornate a room at Westminster as can be found, make appointment to be one of its judges an honour equal to or greater than heading any of the other specialist courts.

The trouble with *Kelly's* proposal of a non-court is that it is very unlikely to be effective because of the rule that any regulatory regime dealing with parliament has to observe the convention that the disciplining of members of the House should be left to the House itself. This is simply wrong. Fraudulent expenses claims should be treated as theft plain and simple, and so the courts, as in any other case about theft, are the appropriate tribunals. Establishing an expert, dedicated court seems entirely sensible, given the complexities of the rules applying to the House of Commons.

Whenever there has been an aspect of the state where careful, even sensitive application of the law has been necessary, we have in the past been equal to the task. The church has its own courts, the military too, and so now must parliament. Having passed the laws by which it intends to abide, these must be enforced by a court formally constituted for that purpose and that purpose alone. This will allow credible expertise to be built up, and should ensure that no partisan temptations will intervene in the administration of justice. Furthermore, far from graduated sanctions being the order of the day, expulsion from the Commons should be a likely punishment (additional to normal penalties for theft) for anything other than technical, genuinely accidental infringements of rules – rules which *Kelly* rightly says should be simple to understand.

What can the case be against creating such a court, heading it with a judge, someone expertly trained to enforce the law, and providing it with a full range of criminal sanctions? One objection, among others, to *Kelly's* proposal to hand investigation and punishment over to the IPSA, is that that particular body's powers will not be clear. We cannot be sure to what degree it will still be subject to the House, through the Committee of Standards and Privileges, for implementation of its rulings, or whether its decisions may be overturned by the Committee. Of course, creating a Court of Parliament actually gives honest MPs *more* protection because it equips them with a clearly defined means of appeal, in addition to the basic fair procedure of a court.

Another virtue of this proposal is that, since by its rules it will be confined to dealing with matters of expenses, it will not intrude into places where IPSA is meant to go. Questions of alleged misbehaviour, such as an MP having lied to the House, or ethical considerations, where a member may have acted improperly (say, by being an undeclared paid lobbyist) would be entirely outside the ambit of this court. Its sole function would be to hear cases of alleged wrongdoing in connection with public monies intended to be given to MPs for their parliamentary functions, and voted for as such by the House. IPSA will only examine matters which should remain the responsibility of MPs themselves to determine.

As things stand, the PSA has created a statutory body, the IPSA, and also the Parliamentary Commissioner for Standards, neither subject to parliamentary privilege. Their work therefore is *potentially* reviewable by the courts. Even though IPSA has been designed not to be a court, the legislation is so loosely drafted that its rulings may end up in the hands of courts. I repeat: by establishing a tightly delineated court as I have outlined above, parliament would be protecting itself.

Numbers talk

Some extensions of what will constitute a criminal act in terms of abusing allowances are intended by the PSA, but most of the behaviour needing to be dealt with was already caught by the criminal law. This is hardly comforting given the small number of prosecutions so far. In practice, IPSA's main sanction will be something like the Legg ultimate penalty: that is, once an MP has been caught and proved to have abused the system, future payments can be withheld until the accounts are back in balance.

As with so much else in British life, the past does offer a guide. Even under the old regime, the Commons was theoretically equipped to deal with flagrant offenders. Although the power to expel has not been used since the case of Gary Allighan in 1947, where the House voted 187-75 to expel him for a breach of privilege (leaking information to journalists) expulsion is one of the punishments MPs need to face, and expect, for venality. A court is the body, in the case of abuse of expenses etc, to decree it.

A generation ago, the American system wrestled with its version of the parliamentary privilege dilemma, and came up with the solution of an independent prosecutor. The Independent, or more recently 'Special', Counsel, was the solution to the Nixon administration's effort to frustrate the progress of the law over Watergate (initially with lines of expenditure, rather than expletives, deleted). For once hyperbole is not misplaced: the expenses scandal of 2009 was the British Watergate, and it requires a solution at least as effective. Watergate cost a head of state his office. Our version has seen a speaker, admittedly far from perfect, serve as scapegoat, but no real reforms. The system remains broken because it suits the people who broke it.

At least the Committee was honest

In disagreeing with some of what *Kelly* recommends, and holding that it fundamentally fails to solve the problem revealed to us, I am not casting doubt on the sincerity or effort of the Committee. Like so much else of the old-fashioned British political system, the CSPL is hard-working, cost-effective and publicly minded. Indeed, there is much to agree with among its recommendations.

A formal 'audit of expenditure' should be introduced into the administration of the House, and it should take great care, in particular, to investigate whether an MP is pushing public resources the way of a political party;[1] receipts for travel should be provided: we cannot, unfortunately, proceed on the assumption that "honourable members" will always be honourable about these matters.

Certainly, suspected abuses in connection with expenses should be pursued in the first instance by outside bodies, but it is hard to see why these should not simply be the police and the CPS; the investigatory authority, whatever it is, has to be able to initiate cases without having to wait for complaints to be made to it. Quarterly, or possibly, every session, full claims (both those met, and those made and rejected) should be published, along with receipts.[2] If MPs want to claim money from us, they have to show us just why they need it. *Kelly*, in many details, is a sensible report. But it omits the question as to why the abuses happened, and they are therefore likely to be repeated. Why should they not be? The same people who abused their allowances will still be with us in large numbers.

Kelly makes sensible, practical suggestions about some matters that should never have arisen in the first place. Hugely expensive electrical equipment, whether for offices or homes, should have remained the property of parliament, assuming they should ever have been bought in the first place. Similarly we should be told how much of their budgets MPs spend.[3] Let them compete in daylight. If some MPs are willing to justify spending every public penny available to them, let them. Others can make the opposite case and the voters can decide. Rightly, league tables are the basis of transparency in the public sector, and are just as applicable to MPs too.

Let me deal with the argument that excessive allowances are justifiable because MPs are paid too little and that they were unable to raise their pay because the public would not wear that. That is utterly wrong. It could not be more wrong. If there is one institution which should be transparent, and should not try to deceive the public in any way, it is parliament itself. To allow excessive allowances as compensation for what MPs claim to be too low a rate of pay is nothing more than an attempt to deceive the public into thinking MPs are getting less than they really are.

I would argue that MPs are not in fact underpaid. I showed the figures to support that argument in Chapter 1, but if, contrary to that view, MPs think that they really are underpaid, they should have the courage to vote for more pay for themselves and to justify that to the public. Let us therefore, in considering the level of any allowance, see whether it should be paid because it is necessary, the test being the statement which MPs have to sign up to every year in respect of accommodation allowances: 'I incurred these costs wholly, exclusively and necessarily to enable me to stay overnight away from my only or main home for the purposes of performing my duties as a member of parliament'.

The Communications Allowance

Let me take one area where I support *Kelly*. The Communications Allowance must go. It has become the way MPs can *advertise* themselves to their constituents at public expense, though theoretically not in a political manner. It is wrong that MPs not only have access to a £10,400 'communications allowance', but that, because they are allowed to switch funds between budget headings, at least 11 MPs managed to spend more than £20,000 from public funds 'communicating' with their voters.[4] This is a waste of public funds, and a significant bias towards incumbency.

It was introduced by Jack Straw in 2007 to deal with the fact that MPs – disproportionately Labour members – were so abusing the free postage traditionally offered to MPs that bills for postage and stationery were being run up in excess of £30,000 per annum. It was thus sold as an economy measure (and the previously unlimited access to postage and Commons stationery was capped at £7,000) when in truth all it was doing, in classic New Labour fashion, was legitimising bad behaviour and moving on. To their credit, the Tories vigorously opposed its introduction at every stage.

To their discredit, however, once the Communications Allowance was introduced, all save twenty one Tory MPs used it. *The Evening Standard* journalist Paul Waugh worked out that members of the shadow cabinet alone were together claiming £186,836. In the wake of the expenses scandal, denouncing it was one of the fleet-footed actions the leader of the opposition was praised for. 'Taxpayers', Mr Cameron said, 'are effectively paying out tens of thousands of pounds so we can all tell our constituents what a wonderful job we are all doing. We've all done it and we all know the facts. It's a gigantic waste of money'.

Indeed, looking round the shadow cabinet table would have reminded him exactly where it was wasted. Michael Gove's £15,705 was the single highest claim. Yet others, not all of whom enjoy such a safe seat as Surrey Heath, ignored it. Dominic Grieve claimed nothing, Nick Herbert merely £323 and William Hague only £336.

Mr Cameron, probably our next Prime Minister, knew that he and his colleagues were wasting public money, and still they did it. Why? Yet what does *Kelly* actually propose? Yes, the Communications Allowance will be abolished, but it proposes that MPs may use public funds to send out such material as before, provided there is a balance left in their allowances to spend on this.[5]

Thus, for *Kelly*, it is a matter of obliging MPs to make a choice as to what they might want to do with 'their' money. It should be a basic principle of British democracy that if an MP wants to communicate with voters, he does so on exactly the same basis as anyone else – out of his own pocket, or from party funds. And the reason, I suggest, why *Kelly* doesn't think the way I do is because we have such very different ideas of what an MP is for.

What is probably the most controversial of allowances is what used to be called the Additional Costs Allowance (ACA) but is now officially called the PAAE (Personal Additional Accommodation Expenditure allowance). Because 'Additional Costs Allowance' describes it much better I shall continue to use that description, or ACA. It was only in 1971 that it was introduced and then it was intended simply to pay for hotel accommodation for those who lived elsewhere but needed to be in London some nights to do their work in Westminster. It has grown astronomically so that it is now a method by which MPs can get mortgages and numerous other substantial expenses paid by the state in order to buy expensive and luxurious homes fitted with expensive television sets and many other luxurious items. There is no way that this can conceivably be justified. It is shocking.

What if the MP decides instead to rent or buy a property? There is certainly an argument that he should get some of the cost so long as it does not exceed what a hotel would have cost. But that is complicated and would be open to abuse, as before. So I believe the answer has to be, hotel stays only, with receipts having to be produced before MPs are refunded the expense they have actually incurred.

So when should MPs be paid any additional accommodation allowance? First of all it is clear that an MP with a constituency in or close to London should have no allowance at all. If he chooses not to live close to where he works, that is his own choice and he should receive no assistance because of it.

An MP with a constituency not within commuting distance of London is obviously in a different situation. An MP's main place of work is Westminster and therefore he should normally have a home in London. If he does so it is clearly reasonable for him to claim for staying in his constituency for a couple of nights a week. If instead he chooses to live in or near his consistency it is still the case that his main place of work is Westminster, but I think it would be reasonable to allow him to charge the same amount as he would have been able to charge had he lived in Westminster and needed to visit his constituency.

MPs on the move

Though provision of housing, as distinct from accommodation, is the source of much of the difficulty, *Kelly* is noticeably wrong-headed on the vexed subject of transport costs.[6] The report concludes that MPs should not be reimbursed for 'ordinary' commuting, and that the purpose and destination of all claimable journeys should be recorded and declared. All sensible enough, but we need to be very careful. There is a case, the further away a constituency is from London, for a travel supplement, for the simple act of getting between Westminster and the seat twice a week (once there, once back). Travel between a seat and Westminster should be an entirely straightforward process, requiring a minimum of administration by the parliamentary authorities.

I risk being seen as a killjoy, but what is the rationale for *Kelly's* 28th Recommendation, providing for the travel costs of an MP's family members? These costs would not normally be provided for those in other occupations and should not be provided for MPs.

Relinquishing the burden

The 30th Recommendation of the Committee supports the current practice of paying MPs a 'resettlement' grant should they be defeated or otherwise 'involuntarily' lose their seats (through a boundary change, for example), as opposed to the eight weeks' pay which retiring MPs get.

At the moment such an MP receives a resettlement grant (intended as redundancy pay) somewhere between £32,383 and £64,766. As with redundancy money in other walks of life, the first £30,000 is tax free. The amount an MP gets is calculated according to the total time spent in parliament, and age on leaving. This scheme was originally introduced in 1971. MPs *also* get a winding up grant, available to them up to 6 months after the election at which they left the House, of up to £42,068. This is calculated as one third of staffing expenditure plus one third of AOE.

The BBC has made the following estimates of the likely resettlement grant for some of the more familiar names of the last year: Derek Conway: £64,766; Douglas Hogg: £59,580; Julie Kirkbride: £32,383; Andrew MacKay: £64,766; Anthony Steen: £32,383; and for Sir Peter Viggers: £32,383.

Among the worst aspects of this system is that, as compared to the two months' pay for retirees, the resettlement grant inescapably provides a direct financial incentive for MPs to 'unnaturally' fight on, regardless of political inclination or circumstances. It should be a rule of the allowances system that it does as little as possible to warp the political situation. Still more to the point, as the TaxPayers' Alliance so rightly pointed out in their evidence to *Kelly*, if MPs insist upon being treated like anyone else, so be it. Anyone who gets elected knows the terms of employment.

The fundamental point, however, as I have already suggested, is that being an MP should not be regarded as a career and therefore there should be no resettlement grant when the MP becomes no longer an MP, whatever the reason. I think two months' pay should apply irrespective of the reason why the MP is no longer an MP.

A hardship scheme for ex-MPs in genuine need would be welcome. It would be an excellent charitable purpose, and many people would probably wish to donate to it: an MP's life, as properly conceived, is one of public service. Mind you, as MPs do so often tell us that being in parliament has 'cost them money', it probably would not be a scheme too many former members would need to turn to.

Kelly appears to see the role of MPs very much through civil service-tinted glasses. This is perhaps most apparent in its attitude towards the function, and nature, of MPs' staff. Far too many MPs have behaved discreditably in the matter of who they employ. Even after frantic changes were made to the staff directory at Westminster in the wake of the Conway revelations, as MPs either shed unfortunate 'employees' or saw them safely transferred to the stewardship of a friendly colleague, almost a third of MPs still employ relatives. Most are spouses, and related employees habitually receive from their members rather higher bonuses than their unrelated co-workers. *Kelly*, as his 15th Recommendation, says it has to stop. Relations can of course continue to work for, and be paid by MPs from their own income, or they can work for their relative, but not be paid for from a parliamentary allowance.

I am in considerable doubt about this. In many ways a ban would be a shame. Large numbers of very good, very dedicated people have served the public at Westminster by working for a husband, wife or parent. But like so much else over the last ten or even twenty years at Westminster, it went wrong. When, in the past, eccentric, or colourful, or even simply very close spouses worked together, that was probably fine. When nearly half the discretionary parliamentary payroll comprised members' relatives, a wearingly familiar lack of propriety had probably occurred. Sadly, for the honest men and woman who used to work this way, the naked greed of others may have ruined it. The innocent may have to suffer with the guilty. If a way can be found, which is not too intrusive, of discovering whether a spouse or other relative really is doing work commensurate with the pay, that will be fine, but I doubt whether that is possible, particularly if it is claimed the work is being done outside the Palace of Westminster.

What, then, should the staff that remain do? *Kelly* inveighs against them performing 'political duties'.[7] I disagree. First, it is the stuff of make-believe. MPs *are* political, and it is because they should and always will be political, that we should honestly acknowledge it of their staff as well, rather than retreating into pretence. My point, however, goes further: we should positively want their staff to be *political*, not in the sense of being servants of a party, but as servants of their member. Restoring the individual MP's own sense of himself as a *private* member would be one of the most effective things real reform could do to the House of Commons. Empowering such MPs means equipping them, if needs be, *against* their own party leaderships and whips. Adequate political staff are invaluable resources, but, like their members, their purpose is to be in Westminster.

MPs' pay

In considering the pay of MPs it is important to question what MPs really ought to be doing. Why should this not be a key matter for public discussion and investigation? I believe, given the enormous sums parliament now costs, that a Royal Commission should examine the role of a modern MP. How much of what they do is make-work? How much is social work, inappropriately and quite likely inefficiently done? How much of it is mere electioneering? Being an MP is *meant* to leave sufficient slack to allow one to take up the demanding role of a minister. It follows that no one can claim that a legislature, only *some* of whose members are intermittent ministers, is a chamber full of 'full time legislators'. In any event, the requirement to legislate should ebb and flow, as with most things in life. One of the worst cultural changes imposed upon parliament by the current government was the idea, inherent in the reform of its working hours by the late Robin Cook, that it was a normal, 'nine to five' workplace with normal, regular working patterns. That thinking may well have contributed to the problems at hand and one is drawn again to the deliberations of Enoch Powell upon the MP as 'full-time employee' in 1971. Why should this not be a key matter for public discussion and investigation?

As I see it, one of the very worst things in *Kelly* is the series of proposals and institutional changes that would deprive MPs of the responsibility for setting their own pay and allowances. As I have already said, MPs must control their own pay so that we can control them. I have little doubt that the cross-party consensus behind *Kelly*, in favour of nominally removing MPs' responsibility for their pay to a third party body, is designed exactly to avoid this popular scrutiny.

At the moment, the Commons regulates itself in respect of the payments of members' salaries and allowances, and the registration and declaration of their financial interests. The purpose of IPSA is to sweep this away. While criminal penalties are provided for, or more precisely, reaffirmed, the main sanction IPSA is intended and expected to use against those who abuse their pay or allowances is, 'a mechanism through which overpayments may be recovered by permitting the setting off of payments to which an MP is not entitled against payments to which the MP is entitled'.[8]

IPSA is intended to 'establish' the allowances' regime, administer the payments to MPs and their staff, hear appeals from MPs against IPSA staff decisions, and investigate relevant complaints made against MPs and their staff. It will also 'administer' MPs' salaries but it will simply pay over the figure determined by the Senior Salaries Review Board (SSRB), and passed on to it by resolution of the House. Here is the thick end of the wedge. Once the SSRB begins merely to relay through the Commons what IPSA should pay MPs, the role of MPs in the matter becomes nugatory. They have an interest, of course, in wishing to see themselves removed by stealth from this process. When we look at how the SSRB arrives at what they should be paid, that is no surprise.

In theory, the SSRB determines an average of a basket of senior civil service grades and uses this as the starting point for the annual increase it recommends for MPs. Prior to the creation of IPSA, these figures were accepted by the Commons without vote or discussion. Plainly, with the existence of such a body as IPSA to report to, all hope of exercising popular control over MPs in this matter will disappear.

The SSRB also made the running in recommending what MPs' various allowances should be. At one of *Kelly's* public hearings, the evidence of senior figures from the SSRB was markedly incoherent. The SSRB's representatives were asked by Sir Christopher Kelly why, for example, the SSRB had recommended that the Additional Costs Allowance should go up to £23,083. Keith Masson replied:

Well, it has been set in the dim and distant past and updated every year by RPI and basically there were a number of bits of evidence; the consultants again looked at it, looked at the cost of maintaining a flat in London, we talked to MPs themselves, some of whom argued that it was not enough, some of whom said it was comfortable.[9]

In recent SSRB reports on MPs' pay, they concluded about the system of which they were such a central part (and remain at least as much so under the IPSA regime) that 'we have received no substantive evidence that MPs are abusing the system'.

In making these points I am not trying to ridicule the conceptual basis for virtually everything the SSRB does, namely the application of 'comparable' rate to the public sector. This is its task, and like a good quango should, it does it to the best of its ability. What astonishes me is that for so long now – more than thirty years – anyone can have believed that it was appropriate for the SSRB to determine the pay of MPs. Like everything else involving MPs, that should be *our* job. We should be the ones telling MPs what they are paid. *Our* recommendation, as expressed through the ballot box, should be the one the House pays heed to.

What has been the result of this steady, stealthy generation's work by MPs to obscure how they are paid? Ever larger salaries; ever more abused allowances. Running through my entire argument is the belief that the truth is the best medicine. If we know what our MPs are doing, and if they are obliged to do it in front of us, so much the better for both us and them.

There is a reason why Britain never developed the continental habit of 'secret sessions' and 'secret budgets'. It is that once upon a time we knew that in dark places bad things happen. We should never have allowed MPs to do bad things to themselves, but we can have no confidence that IPSA will in any way aid transparency or disinfect with sunlight. *Kelly* holds that a great boon which IPSA will help to achieve is that MPs will be better 'protected' against governments who might otherwise have imposed lower salary settlements than those the SSRB recommended, for 'political reasons'.[10] But if MPs want to rebuff such a move, they have the remedy in their own hands – as long as they are still involved in the process. Turning MPs into passive household pets, patted and fed and watered, is exactly the way to render them docile in every other regard too.

MPs' pensions

Though *Kelly* prudently disavowed pronouncing on salary or allowance levels[11] (which undoubtedly saved the Committee much anguish with the public and the press) this left an enormous hole in the report: that is, the enormous cost of MPs' pensions. This huge sum (31% to the Exchequer, reduced temporarily to 26.5%) is incomprehensible by private sector comparisons.

Here, unaddressed by *Kelly*, is the need to make a clean break with the past. Almost half the population have no pension other that the state one; for those with private pensions, a 6% contribution would be gratifying, and a fully funded final salary scheme would be like water in the desert. These treats do not, however, stop here. For almost everyone other than MPs, forty long years are needed to get to the maximum allowed figure of two thirds of your final salary for a pension. MPs allow themselves to receive that pension after a mere twenty-five years. This was justified on the basis of the volatility of being an MP – the year used to illustrate this was the exceptional election of 1997.

And there is more – ministerial and 'office holders' (the latterly salaried chairmen of committees mostly) receive, of course, a top-up for the period of ministerial or officerial service. As you might by now have expected, the Commons has brought a particular refinement to this. If you were, for example, a minister for five years out of your quarter century in the House, you get the ministerial section of your pension not as per the rate prevailing for the period for when you actually were a minister, but as per current ministerial salaries at the time you receive your pension.

Kelly has avoided the pension question, but we should not. Action needs to be taken, and immediately – before the end of this parliament, otherwise we could end up with nearly 300 new claimants, all benefiting from the old regime. During the worst economic downturn since the Great Depression, when other countries are imposing swingeing cuts to their public payrolls, our MPs should be setting an example, not looking for new ways to dress up old demands.

4.
Naught but a bauble?

When illusions were revealed

The global and British economies are back in growth. In the UK's case, this amounts to no more than a mere 0.1%. At first sight this would seem to have vindicated the path that the British government, and indeed, most governments, have followed. I believe, however, that this policy response has merely postponed the resolution of significant underlying structural problems in the British economy, many of which have gone almost unchallenged over the last decade.

In the UK, unemployment has levelled off well below the three million many economists predicted, asset prices have firmed up (the FTSE 100 has increased by over 40% since its March 2009 low), house prices (as measured by the Halifax House Price Index) have risen for six months in a row, and the British Retail Consortium has reported Christmas like-for-like trading up a healthy 4.2%.

Twelve months ago the world looked very different, as first domestic then global banks were rescued, global trade contracted at an unprecedented post-war rate and the very stability of the international financial system was questioned.

What went wrong?

Before considering the policy response we need to understand what caused this crisis. Was it those popular scapegoats, the bankers, who wrecked the economy, or perhaps governments or maybe even us, the consumer? For if we do not understand the real underlying causes of the problem we are unlikely to come to the correct conclusions as to the remedy.

I believe that the banking crisis was a symptom of the problem, not the cause. It is easy to blame the bankers and indeed in many cases there was excess, but the underlying cause was inappropriate global and domestic monetary policy, which encouraged credit expansion. The UK government instigated targeting of the Bank of England was too narrow in focusing on the Consumer Price Index without any reference to asset price inflation or banking leverage. Further, as I will explore in more detail below, the extraordinary state-sponsored expansion of the public sector, which crowded out the private sector, was a major contributory factor to an unsustainable and reckless boom.

If we understand the causes of the problem, only then can a proper diagnosis and cure be attempted. The government and opposition have both taken the easy option – blame the greedy global bankers – when a diagnosis closer to home would have been more honest.

In the last decade, in fact, ever since the UK's escape from the ERM, Britain's record of GDP growth consistently exceeded Europe's growth. Pointedly so in the case of France, Germany and Italy. Britain prided itself on open markets, low regulation and a relatively benign tax regime. This happy self-image was, in my opinion, the rose-tinted aftermath of the economic reforms of the 1980s and 1990s. For while in reality markets remained open, both regulation and taxation increased markedly over the last decade, as did public expenditure and leverage – both private and public. The UK's growth was increasingly driven by unsustainable factors which, if not reversed, will undermine our long term potential for recovery.

Undoing the good work

One of my central themes is that as the UK's economic advantages were eroded, growth was based on a number of one-off factors and the underlying economy became unbalanced: biased towards property, finance and the public sector, all fuelled by an increasing and very high level of debt. Given the current policy response, repeating our recent growth rate over the next decade looks a much tougher challenge as the UK faces some substantial structural headwinds.

The Treasury has forecast a fairly low level of GDP growth in 2010 (1.25% to 1.75%) followed by a rapid and sustained recovery with annualised increases in GDP anticipated at well over 3% from 2011 onward. Unless there is substantial reform and a changed economic direction I believe that this forecast will prove grossly optimistic. This matters, not just for economic growth, but also because the public sector deficit is considerably more entrenched than the consensus currently believes, and lower growth will impact tax revenues.

During the last decade, bank leverage increased markedly. Total outstanding loans increased from £3.9tn in 2004 peaking at £9tn in 2008 – or approximately six times GDP. This figure has subsequently contracted to £7.5tn (with a substantial unwinding of derivative positions and more importantly a 7% contraction in outstanding loans to customers) but undoubtedly this expansion in credit significantly boosted

GDP through the decade. While the partial recapitalisation of the banking sector and the impact of quantitative easing will have helped the medium term lending environment, overall lending growth should be assumed to be muted. The example of Japan bears testimony to what happens to corporate lending in a low growth, deflationary environment. This is our first great problem.

Second is the fact that the make-up of the UK economy has been evolving rapidly. In 1978, 26% of the population worked in manufacturing. The comparable figure today is 8.9%. Similarly, over that period the proportion working in banking and finance rose from 10.5% to 20.1%. The rise in public sector employment has also been significant, particularly over the last decade, with an additional one million direct public sector jobs 'created', taking the current total to 6.1m. This underestimates the importance of the state given the growth in the state dependent sector, be it through outsourcing or regulation. The economy has thus become increasingly focused on banking, finance and the public sector. The manufacturing base is now relatively small, and although it should benefit from sterling depreciation, it is no longer significant enough to drive domestic GDP growth, in the short term at least. This sectoral bias aided growth in the last decade. It is unlikely to be so positive in the next.

Our third main problem comes when we examine public expenditure trends closely. It is apparent that there has been a very substantial public sector pump-priming spend which is both undesirable and unsustainable. This point seemed to be completely lost on most economic and political commentators. Certainly any belief that 'the proceeds of growth' could be shared with the public sector was to misunderstand both the fundamental long term growth dynamics and the sustainability of such spending.

From 2000/1 to 2008/9, public spending increased from £364bn to £617bn. The current Treasury forecast is for £702bn of spending by 2010/11. Taking the population as 60m, this implies that spending has increased from £6,050 a head to around £10,250 over this period and is forecast to be £11,700 by 2011. This was over a period of relatively low inflation. If the public sector had grown in line with the CPI increase, by 2009 spending would have been around £120bn lower or £85bn lower if spending had risen in line with GDP. For comparison, £85bn is equivalent to the entire current education budget.

Government spending as a proportion of GDP has increased from 36.8% in 2000 to 43.2% today. Given the recession in the private sector alongside continuing accelerated public spending, the figure will likely be 48% of GDP by the end of this financial year. This is back to levels last seen in the mid 1970s. The impact on crowding out the private sector is potentially profound. It has been estimated that pump-priming increased growth, albeit in an unsustainable way, by 1% p.a. for the last decade. As a cross-check to these claims of overspend, we should note that if the government had observed a criterion of 3% deficit spending, a cut of around £130bn would now be required.

Refusing to face reality

Although the government and opposition have started a debate on reducing the deficit, with Labour pledging to halve the deficit over 4 years, there is a lack of reality about the action required. The Treasury forecasts a deficit of £175bn for the current fiscal year. This is almost twice as bad in percentage terms as Britain's deficit during the height of the IMF crisis of the mid 1970s.

The nature of this crisis and the emergency monetary and fiscal policy has meant that it has been a strange recession for those remaining in employment. Disposable income has, in aggregate, increased. The public as a whole seem unprepared for what is required if the finances of the economy are to be stabilised. There are major political risks attached to this, for if the population as a whole is unfamiliar, or unaware, of the measures necessary to stabilise the economy, the political consequences could be severe. Honesty is required, with a firm and well thought out plan to cut the deficit in the short term in order to provide a sustainable platform for future growth. Neither of the two major parties are showing much long term thinking or proposing a sustainable strategy.

There are effectively three ways of tackling the deficit. The first is to allow tax receipts to erode the deficit by stimulating GDP growth. This has been the Labour government's primary approach. And the results are plain to see: 0.1% growth in Q4. Those who believe in this generally subscribe to the view that the deficit is largely cyclical. I believe that the dynamics for growth are now largely absent. Artificial stimulation is little more than fool's gold.

The choice is thus unpalatable. Tax rises or spending cuts? If the UK is to rebuild long term economic growth there is no choice but to cut the excess spending of the last decade, and cut it very significantly. To raise taxes will be counter-productive. The UK's tax advantage over most of our European competitors has already been lost. Further tax rises will be counter-productive and will further erode the UK's competitive position.

Furthermore, it is simply not credible to ringfence large proportions of public spending from proposed cuts. If health, international development and presumably large parts of social protection are ringfenced, this, coupled with the rising debt repayment burden, must mean that the weight of cuts on education, defence and infrastructure spend will be enormous. I believe that, as a minimum, £60 to 80bn of cuts will be required over the next three fiscal years. That is around 10% to 12% of the entire public sector budget. No departments should be exempt. Given the unparalleled growth in spending, cuts of this magnitude should be achievable without significantly impacting upon services: there is fat to trim. The health budget, for example, increased from £54.2bn in 2000/1 to £109.9bn in 2008/9 without markedly increasing positive health outcomes. A similar case can be made with education. Are we really as a country so much better educated now that that budget has increased from £45.9bn to £81.4bn during the same period?

The rise in UK debt is extraordinary and it is to the shame of the country that the issue has been barely debated in parliament. The accumulated national debt since the Napoleonic Wars breached £400bn in October 2004. Five years later, it had more than doubled reaching £844bn in November 2009. Using the Treasury's own forecast, debt will reach £1.59tn by 2013/14. Currently refinancing the 10 year gilt costs HMG around 3.9%. If refinancing costs stay the same (and this is not a given) debt repayment costs will rise from a current £33bn to around £70bn by 2014. This will compound the cuts required elsewhere in the economy.

The real situation is substantially worse than this, for the Treasury's numbers exclude around £150bn of PFI (largely accumulated over the last decade) and according to the PBR, an actuarial assumption of £810bn of unfunded state pension obligations as well. Using Treasury forecasts, and the central actuarial forecast for pensions, total state debt by 2013/4 will be in the region of £2.55tn. Or around 160% of GDP, which amounts to £42.5k a head. Short term political expediency has triumphed over long term prudence and neither the government nor the opposition seems to have noticed.

We need to act

There is no free lunch, as spending cuts in the short term will impact tax revenues and government growth assumptions, while tax rises would also crowd out the private sector. There is no painless choice. The historic tragedy, dating back to the early 2000s, is the lack of opposition to these reckless spending priorities of the current government. In an attempt to look moderate and modern, the Conservative party missed the big picture, that Brown's economy was an unsustainable engine for growth.

The deficit remains critical, however, for the very stability of the nation. Bond and currency markets understand that we are in a pre-election phoney war. After the election, great determination will be needed to tackle the UK's greatest structural weakness. Failure to articulate a credible and urgent plan will engender prolonged currency weakness and very likely a spiralling of interest rates. Such an outcome would be catastrophic for the UK. It is not too harsh to cut spending now, because not doing so will have a much harsher impact on the economy and public spending in the future.

International investors place critical importance on government bond markets. If the market suffers a loss of confidence and demands a higher yield on government debt, what price UK real estate? That is why doing nothing, in terms of government borrowing, is not an option for British policy makers.

The UK has faced many crises before. This economic crisis is, I believe, of critical importance. State growth is out of control, the public sector remains unionised and leverage is at critical levels. The populace seems oblivious to the dangers ahead – chiefly because the opposition has not opposed. The Tory party has not performed its public duty: to explain the nature of the crisis and to offer a viable, long term vision for the future. On top of this, the new government will be constrained, to a much greater extent than the Thatcher administration, by EU regulation and law.

However, I believe that there is a positive route map than can turn the UK around and put the economy on a long term sustainable growth path. Undoing the unproductive growth in the state and arresting the impact of the inevitable unwinding of the fiscal and monetary stimulus will take time, but the roots of recovery can be achieved within the framework of a five year parliament.

A road to recovery

First, the deficit must be tackled. The penalty for not doing so is too great. The next government will inherit substantial headwinds and must act immediately on the deficit and stabilise long term interest rates. No areas of the budget should be ringfenced but priority should be given to infrastructure and defence, which are both of long term strategic importance to the nation. No cuts programme can exempt social protection and healthcare from efficiency savings and re-organisation.

Second, a medium term plan for five years and ten years should be established to reduce the size of the state, which now accounts for almost half the UK economy. Progress will be dependent on growth, but no economy can successfully grow in the long term with such dependence on the state. I propose that a target of 40% be set for 2015 and 36% to 2020. This would merely take the economy back to the levels of state dependency where Labour had them in 2000/01.

Third, as a quid pro quo for outlining a plan towards fiscal stability, it should be easier to maintain rates close to 0.5%. While this will be the Bank of England's responsibility, the maintenance of very low rates will help provide an environment for investment.

Fourth, the Monetary Policy Committee's remit should be widened. The government target of tracking CPI is too narrow and has led to distortions in the economy. The MPC should keep its independence but be tasked with tracking a wide range of measures including CPI, RPI, the M4 money supply, asset price inflation (property in particular) and major bank leverage. Powers to extend quantitative easing should be granted when a broad range of measures indicate its appropriate use.

Fifth, regulation has been overly focused on the minutiae and has missed the big picture. Going forward, regulation should allow for minimal day to day interference but monitor big picture risks, particularly overall banking system leverage and systemic risk.

Sixth, unfunded public sector pensions need to be reformed. The only chance of doing this is during a financial crisis. On current actuarial assumptions, £810bn of state obligations are unfunded. The gap between public and private sector pensions is unsustainable. The public sector retirement age should be increased from 60 to 65 with an escalator to 67 as the pension retirement age is raised. Existing benefits should be honoured, but henceforth a pay-as-you-go scheme should be implemented, and partially funded by the state with employee top-ups.

Seventh, public sector national pay bargaining should be abolished. Public sector pay should mirror local conditions. This would break the power of public sector unions while making pay much more responsive to the market.

Eighth, 'sharing the proceeds for growth' is off the agenda for good. We need a long term plan to stimulate the private sector and shrink the state which now accounts for 48% of GDP. This can only be achieved by creating a low regulation, low tax environment in the long term. The government needs to tackle EU regulation in general and in particular the EU's new authority over the City. The French would not allow viniculture to be dominated by the British in the way that we have surrendered regulatory authority over the City. There needs to be action on this front; not words, nor even cast-iron guarantees.

And last of all, Britain needs an alternative. Being a lighter shade of red will neither save the economy nor impress the electorate.

5.
Wrong and getting worse

The 'Founding Fathers of the European Union' wanted to prevent another European war – obviously a good motive. But there was another motive, too – a secret one – and, as early as 1952, Jean Monnet made it clear for those who would listen: 'Europe's nations should be guided towards the super-state without the people understanding what is happening. This can be accomplished by successive steps, each disguised as having an economic purpose, but which will eventually and irreversibly lead to federation'. How very clear and how very accurate! Our own entry into the EU, I have to say, involved our politicians telling lies, and so did the handling of the Lisbon Treaty.

Mr Heath and the truth

Edward Heath was much less than honest with the British people. Compare two of his statements. In 1966 he said, 'We should frankly recognise this surrender of sovereignty and its purpose'. In 1973, however, when he was trying to get our voters to say Yes to staying in, he said, 'There are some in this country who fear that in going into Europe we shall in some way sacrifice independence and sovereignty...these fears, I need hardly say, are completely unjustified'.

He allowed himself, moreover, to be blackmailed over the Common Fisheries Policy, which has destroyed our once great fishing industry. Norway and the UK, both applying for membership at the same time, were confronted with this 'policy' at the last moment and told that they must sign or stay out. We signed. Norway refused, has stayed out, and is one of the two countries in the whole EU area with the highest GDP per capita (except tiny Luxembourg). The other is Switzerland, also not in the EU. These two countries are the only ones in the region not to have joined. Special cases? To some extent, yes – but it is rather striking.

Although it is far from comparing like with like, a useful historical parallel can perhaps be made by comparing the process of joining the EU with the process of appeasement. Appeasers were not bad people, and for a while they formed a popular majority. These were the men and women who had lived through the carnage of the Great War and its aftermath, and quite naturally they wanted no more war, no more post-war chaos and slump. Their answer was to buy off the barbarian at the gate. Of course, we know that that Danegeld did not work.

Trade, protectionism and regulation

The European Community that was built in the 1950s was founded on trade. No other option was available, once the French had rebuffed a military union with a rearmed West Germany. Although we think today in terms of a political EU, remember that before the Treaty of Lisbon came the Single Market and, two decades before that, the Common Market. Butter and lamb were the dominant areas of discussion amid the million words thrown up in the British accession debate in 1972. The Common Market was meant to mean, essentially, a bigger home market, with fewer, and lower, tariffs. It was intended to mean less red tape, at least as far as the man in the lorry cab was concerned.

A closed shop

The Common Market was also, unfortunately, about getting round the threat of protectionism by itself becoming part of the protection racket. As global free trade took off, and India and China began their huge moves forward, Europe remained confined within a tariff zone, hiding behind the sofa. Had it not been for Thatcher and Kohl, the EU today would be languishing inside a bankrupted, autarkic customs union. The Single Market did inject some missing magic and perhaps, for a decade, it rescued the EU. However, it came with a very heavy price: more political integration, extra regulatory burdens, and greater costs.

Consider for a moment what membership of this trading bloc means for a member state today. Rather than simply allowing our goods and services access to other markets, as a manufacturer in Toronto might expect under NAFTA for his products going to Chicago, a bristling hedge of rules funnel the European exporter – 105,000 pages of them, at the last count. Brussels regulates the blueprint rather than simply recognising the product. It is no surprise that ASEAN, the current hub of world growth, has rejected this model.

Turning the supertanker

Trying to rewind or even to ride this process is now impossible. Treaty after treaty has handed over more and more powers, so that the latest one – the Lisbon Treaty – now even contains what Labour MP Gisela Stuart has aptly called 'a competence to create competences'. This so-called *passerelle* clause is merely the latest example of the trend to hand over power and abrogate responsibility. Worse still, it is an accelerating tendency.

As the Bruges Group has observed, the Treaty of Rome provided the groundwork for 38 vetoes to be eventually surrendered. The Single European Act added another 12. Maastricht added another 30. Amsterdam provided for another 24; Nice a further 46; and the EU Constitution would have added a further 68 (the jury is still out on the technicalities of the Lisbon tally). Perhaps it is enough simply to note that, under Tony Blair, more vetoes were surrendered than under all of his predecessors combined. That is as much an indictment of the Labour government and the current Foreign Office as it is an observation of the undeniable acceleration of the process.

The ratchet effect at work

That bald tally leaves entirely to one side the issue of competences, however – the areas in which the EU has inveigled a right, and then an increased right, to legislate in areas formerly the preserve of the nation state. The trend is easy to see. First, the area open to the ratchet effect tends to be an area of interest, of voluntary co-ordination and recommendation; then a budget is attached; then it becomes a joint competence; finally, it becomes an exclusive competence reserved to Brussels.

In practical terms, it means, for instance, that the UK has been collectivised on the world stage. We no longer have an individual say in the WTO, just as our vote was subsumed with other European maritime nations into a single Commission vote for the North West Atlantic Fisheries Organisation. This tendency to turn the Foreign Office into a local branch of Brussels Inc. can only now accelerate with the formal and legal identity provided to the EU Foreign Ministry, which had already existed for a long time in shadowy form, doling out grants to universities that teach Australians about European integration, or defending the intricacies of Europe's beef tariffs before US congressmen.

There is little from the track record of the EU's development budget to suggest that they will make less of a mess of it than they have over the other communitarised policies.

The Common Fisheries Policy and Tory shame

The Common Fisheries Policy ought to be the most infamous example of just how badly managed EU policies can be in Brussels. It is the most disgraceful example of institutionalised ecological pillaging, yet everyone involved in its administration recognises that fact without acting upon it, despite the EU's Green rhetoric.

This demonstrates the bleak failures of the Brussels system. To its credit, the Conservative Front Bench under Patrick Nicholls, Owen Paterson, John Hayes and Ann Winterton won their party round to the revolutionary policy of scrapping the CFP, whatever the repercussions for Britain's relations with the EU. Sadly, that commitment seems now to have been feebly dropped – and, if that is the case, it will prove an abject surrender by that party, and another hammer blow to our ports and harbours.

As far as I am aware, there has only been one major attempt to make a broad calculation of the cost of the damage caused by the CFP. In early 2009, the TaxPayers' Alliance looked at the economic cost of the dumping of hundreds of thousands of dead fish back into the sea, and added to it the wreck of the British fishing fleet, the decay of our coastal communities, and even the impact upon the retail price of the commodity. The figure that resulted was a shocking £2.8 billion a year, with the majority being the cost of the lost resource – that is to say, the loss arising from the surrendering of fishing rights to other EU fishermen, rather than following the example of the Norwegians and Icelanders and keeping our once-rich national waters for the local boats. It is a bitter truth that the British taxpayer has, in effect, subsidised foreign trawler skippers to the tune of hundreds of millions of pounds.

Squandering these stocks has driven the trawlers elsewhere. The tragedy is perhaps most felt in the Third World. For a number of years, reports have been filtering back about the EU's opaque and secretive third-party fisheries agreements. These typically involve poor countries, desperate for cash, and prepared to sell the interest of their coastal communities to get it. Hence, modern Spanish trawlers have appeared off Mauritania and other distant shores, hoovering up resources that were previously sustaining low-yield traditional fishing. This drives the local fishermen out of work – and perhaps contributes in a small way to the migration pressures of which the Spanish themselves so often complain. Worse still, there have been reports of 'black' (or illegal) fishing by trawlers operating without lights, running down local skiffs in the scramble to cram their holds at all costs. In a nutshell, the saga encapsulates much that is wrong with the protectionist, self-centred EU's trade mentality.

French fears about the Anglo-Saxon model

Would that the CFP were the only policy leading to wrong done in the name of Brussels. The French, in particular, have had their eye on perfidious Anglo-Saxon capitalism for some time, and the banking crisis has given them the excuse they need to hobble an economic competitor to the Bourse.

In the wake of a Directive on investment funds, the EU will now bring its weight to bear on the City. Some of the more unthinking commentators will provide knee-jerk support for such a move. It is true that there have been both fools and knaves in the Square Mile over the past few years. But while banks, credit agencies and regulators – though not hedge funds and private equity – must share some of the blame for the recent disasters, the real villain lies elsewhere. As Chapter 4 detailed, the primary responsibility for the credit crunch lies with the governments and central banks that pursued woefully inappropriate monetary policies.

In the meantime, pension funds seem set to be hit by compliance costs running into billions of pounds. Why? Thanks to the EU, of course. And this will be exacerbated because our own government signed up to a Directive that will be extremely damaging to the financial interests of British pensioners. Why did a British government do such an unhelpful thing? To secure 'alliances' that would help it fight other QMV battles in Brussels.

Defending Europe

Then there is the matter of the EU's military ambitions. Having kept the peace among its members for five decades, NATO suffered a minor identity crisis at the end of the Cold War. Paris made moves to exploit this blip, both by bilateral arrangements (such as the St Malô Accords of 1998 with Britain, involving common defence arrangements), and by pushing a separate European defence identity. Rearguard actions by Atlanticist countries such as The Netherlands have only slowed, not halted, the trend.

Under the Lisbon Treaty, and building on its predecessors, the EU now has an astonishing mutual defence commitment: the progressive framing of a Common Defence Policy that 'will lead to a common defence'. There are very vague clauses relating to combating terrorism, and the perilous catch-all of 'peace-making' provides further scope for the EU to play its familiar routine of getting a foot in the door, and pushing ever harder.

The Lisbon Treaty also pushes further the dangerous trap of a European defence agency. One would think that after the shenanigans of the Belgian ammunition embargo during the First Gulf War, the division over the recognition of various post-Yugoslav states, splits over deployments in Iraq and Afghanistan, the A400M military Airbus fiasco, Eurofighter, the Horizon frigate, Galileo, and the FRES logistics scandal, that lessons would by now have been learned. Apparently not.

The appalling, unknown cost of EU membership

These costly fiascos lead us on to question the financial burdens. If Britain joined the EEC in order to boost its trade and to make money, then surely our ledger book must be in the black? With formal EU accounts uncertified for a shocking 14 years, it is hard to obtain an accurate picture. On the two occasions HM Treasury began to do the arithmetic, ministerial orders came from on high to close down the exercise pronto. This rather suggests that the calculations that have been made over the last decade or so by a group of economists from Bradford University, Professor Minford (a former 'Wise Man' to a past chancellor), Ian Milne from the think-tank Global Vision, the Open Europe mathematicians, and by the team from the TaxPayers' Alliance – all of which point to the truly staggering volume of red ink involved in British membership – are correct.

It is indisputably the case that the current net deficit, purely in terms of the direct cost, is running at £6.5 billion annually, and set to go up thanks to Prime Minister Blair giving away part of the Thatcher Rebate. It is also clear that gross contributions (a quarter of a trillion pounds to date by the UK, around £81 billion net) do not always come back to the UK to be spent wisely. These loudly proclaimed fruits of 'European' investment habitually have very tight, very complex strings attached. Also worth bearing in mind is the waste involved in transferring funds from Britain to Britain, via Brussels.

But there is another, hidden, cost as well. For the sake of the proportion of British exports that goes to the EU, all British businesses have to bear the red-tape burden. Estimates of this cost reach perhaps £100 billion or higher; we simply do not know. One Commissioner put the bill at €600 billion across the EU in 2006, and is doubtless higher now. So, even on a conservative estimate, the cost of EU red tape to the UK economy is (since our GDP is around 15% of the EU total) running at roughly £75 billion a year. If the reality lies between the two, it is the equivalent of a Royal Bank of Scotland/Lloyds Banking Group share buyout every year. There is no plausible relief in sight.

This can be put into context by expressing it slightly differently. The cost of the red tape meant to facilitate British exports is about the same as the actual value of the exports themselves. That is an economic nonsense worthy of the pages of Voltaire or Jonathan Swift! It is one that is felt, imperceptibly, by every family in the land, because even at a time of high global food prices that shrink the effects of the CAP, every household is paying an extra £400 a year in higher food bills. As food is a necessity and not a luxury, the poorest families are correspondingly hit hardest.

Such costs do not even begin to reflect the impact of the free transit of the workforce from one country to another. While there is much to commend fluidity where skills are short, and while such policies can encourage competitiveness among the existing domestic workforce, the British government's laissez-faire attitude (required by treaty but bizarrely accelerated voluntarily by ministers) has also created a dangerous backlash.

The truth behind the policy is that, in modelling the EU on other federal states such as the US, Brussels has pushed for increased workforce mobility to accompany a single currency. There is not yet a major sink fund allowing the transfer of federal funds to assist regions facing an economic downturn (a UK parallel is the British government's support of the regeneration of central Liverpool). Other mechanisms are therefore needed to release economic pressure in a currency area, and migration is just such a key mechanism.

The crucial point, which the Conservatives especially need to appreciate, is that the EU problem is not one to be left on one side while the next Prime Minister attends to 'more important' matters such as the financial crisis, health and education. He must take drastic action over the EU or he will never be able to solve the financial crisis or find the resources to devote to our other problems.

The irony is that nationals from EU states that are outside the Eurozone – Eastern Europe – have, quite understandably, when the pound was strong, seized the opportunity to come to Britain, also outside the Eurozone, to earn valuable pounds. The compounding problem is that the British government has already lost its grip on managing the migration flows that we are currently experiencing.

A recent parliamentary question reveals that no less than 24% of the workforce in London, and 8% of the total national workforce, are non-UK nationals. From a purely sociological standpoint, however much one might appreciate cultural diversity, this level can surely not be sustainable over the long term without a heavy social, perhaps even political, cost. The case of the Lindsey oil refinery provides some pointers.

Melting cast-iron guarantees

However, none of these problems can be addressed without taking a radical approach. All three main political parties in the UK pledged a referendum on our relationship with the EU. Labour backtracked on it because it knew it would lose it, and mocked the electorate with the fallacy that the EU Constitution and the Lisbon Treaty were not the same thing. The Conservative party merged muddle with bravado, and have backtracked on the grounds that they will now attempt to tinker with the administration rather than addressing what the 40-year-old facts about EU membership unambiguously mean.

The Liberal Democrats behaved ridiculously over Lisbon. In the House of Commons they instructed their members, by three-line whip, to abstain. Then, in the House of Lords, they instructed their peers to vote in favour of ratification.

Meanwhile, I lost my battle to force the government, through the courts, to hold a referendum. I did, however, receive many gratifying messages of support from the public, including a number of pensioners.

The Lisbon Treaty is such a betrayal of European democracy that it deserves to be thoroughly unpicked and unravelled. Heads of government told the drafters of the EU Constitution to fix the EU's problems, to sort out a system that kept being rejected by the voters of referenda, and to 'bring Europe closer to its citizens'. They did none of that. Instead, what became Lisbon brought more integration, with more power dragged away from the citizens, and the awarding of a legal existence for the EU in its own right. If we do not get the referendum we were promised, we will, sooner rather than later, have to deal with the problems that the EU, and too many of our own politicians, have purposely ignored.

I believe that an honest cost–benefit analysis of EU membership is long overdue. For the political parties, it has the advantage of being a minimal cost pledge whose results would only be felt after the next general election. For the country, it has the boon that it would effectively settle a national controversy that has riven the political scene for four decades. Why should anyone be afraid of hearing the truth about what British membership of the EU, as currently constituted, costs us?

Following a review of our bills, we could then turn to look at fixing the deficit. I suspect that the figures will show a massive negative. Whatever the figures, though, it will only be when the country is presented with an audit that we will be able to clean up our act. A determined effort of massive renegotiation would have to follow. The clarity of the costs would provide both the impetus for our negotiations, and the basis for substantial domestic support for such a programme.

I do not necessarily want to leave the EU: there are problems and issues if we do. But, unlike the more blinkered advocates of membership-come-what-may, I do not intend to shut my eyes to the awkward aspects of membership that I have discussed in this chapter. But we simply cannot continue in the sort of relationship with the EU with which the UK currently suffers. We certainly do not, as a nation, approve of the destination in which the EU is implacably proceeding. Almost all our elected politicians give rhetorical support to the principle that we should not be subsumed inside a European superstate but, bar Mrs Thatcher, none of their practical actions in office ever did a thing to stop it.

We have sincerely tried reform and failed. We have sought change and been blocked. We have protested our anger and been ignored. There comes a time when such things must end. If it comes to it, and we are better off out, then out is where we must be. But that will not be our choice. If it happens, and it may do so sooner than most people think, it will be because Brussels will have driven us out by mistake, arrogantly assuming that their bluff would never be called. Much like MPs, the EU needs to be saved from itself.

6.
Mad or just too hot?

The 2009 UN Conference on Climate Change in Copenhagen was billed as the most important world conference ever. Had it succeeded in reaching a binding agreement along the lines of that called for by those worried about global warming, it might well have been the conference at which the most catastrophic decisions ever had been taken. Those decisions would also, if they had not been so disastrous, have been the most ludicrous of all time.

I have little doubt that by 2050 or, I hope, very much earlier, the early 2000s will be looked back on in amazement as the period in which the world went mad. Very fortunately, the conference reached, to all intents and purposes, no serious deal at all.

It may seem arrogant for someone who is neither a climate scientist nor an economist to have reached as strong a view as I have. It is, however, my considered opinion that what the alarmists, as I shall call them, are hoping to do – and have unfortunately already started to do – is calamitous, and also that their methods are shocking. However, it is, I believe, important to make the point that, disgracefully though some recent revelations have shown a number of scientists to have behaved, the argument against global warming alarmism did not need the revelations in order to be convincing.

Previous Cassandras

You might think that the following document supported the alarmists: a high-priority government report warning of climate change that would lead to floods and starvation. 'Leading climatologists speak of a detrimental global climate change, threatening the stability of most nations.' The usual disasters were predicted.

The 'new climatic era' was said to be bringing famine, starvation, refugee crises, floods, droughts, crop and monsoon failures, and all sorts of extreme weather phenomena. Some readers will not have been alive at the time that this was written:

1974. And the imminent disaster at that time was...a new Ice Age. Even the most eminent scientists were apt to get things a bit wrong.

They got it badly wrong again, moreover, in 1998, after that year had been shown to be the hottest for some time. All the very complicated models constructed by the alarmist scientists predicted that the warming would continue. However, no further global warming has been recorded in the period since 1998 – the world is, instead, cooler now than it then was – and it has never at any point reached the 1998 temperatures.

Lies for war and lies for mass impoverishment

In the UK Tony Blair got the country to go to war by asserting that Saddam Hussein could, within 45 minutes, launch an attack on the UK with nuclear weapons. I do not doubt that Tony Blair thought that invading Iraq was the right thing to do. That certainly did not, however, justify his wild exaggerations to our parliament and our country in order to take us into war.

Turning to climate change, let us consider what P.O. Jones of the University of East Anglia was found to have done even before any of the infamous Climate Research Unit (CRU) emails were revealed. He had refused for 17 years to give the data on which his opinions were based. When asked for a copy of the primary data about temperature he said, 'Why should I make the data available to you, when your aim is to find something wrong with it?' This is not the way scientists should behave. So it was not surprising to learn that crucial data for earlier years had been lost, and that the recent emails revealed continuing resistance to balance, openness and disclosure, with clear manipulation of what data there was.

Then there is Michael Mann's notorious hockey-stick diagram. This purported to show that northern-hemisphere temperatures underwent very little in the way of change for about 1,000 years, only to go up at a startling rate in the last 100 years – so startling that the diagram as a whole looked like a hockey stick. His methods have been found to be completely unreliable, not least because it has been shown that the method employed could have made any set of random data show a hockey-stick picture.

These things do rank, as I see it, as being as serious as Tony Blair's untrustworthy performance over weapons of mass destruction. You may say that something that can lead to a war is much more important than mistaken policies that lead to drastic action on supposedly harmful global warming. That is not so obvious to me. The costs of the measures that have been taken to deal with the alleged problem, and which are proposed for the future, could prove to be so enormous that the bill may well cause the impoverishment, misery and, in many cases, the deaths of hundreds of millions of people. Deception that may have this effect has to be considered as very important indeed and, as I see it, wicked.

Lord Lawson put it well in his excellent book, *An Appeal to Reason: A Cool Look at Global Warming*[1], when referring to the three 'Big Lies' most commonly put forward by alarmists. These are that the science is certain and settled, that global warming is happening, and that carbon dioxide pollutes the atmosphere. As the former chancellor said, it 'is helpful to know that if you read any press report, or hear any politician, giving houseroom to any one of these, let alone all three, you would be well advised to disregard anything else they may say or write on the subject'.[2]

Even *The Economist*, a paper that worries a great deal about global warming, says of the authors of the leaked CRU emails: 'they believe in global warming too much and their commitment to the cause leads them to tolerate poor scientific practice, to close themselves off from criticism, and to deny reasonable requests for data'.

The cost of mitigation

As I understand it, what it is hoped that China will consistently and honestly do, for example, will voluntarily cost that country something like $400 billion, in current terms, by 2020. That is an impressive thing to believe in.

To bring this closer to home, I was sitting not so long ago in a think-tank where the question under discussion was how to make sure we fulfilled our obligation to the EU to produce 20% of our energy from renewables by 2020. I cannot quote anything because the meeting was held under the Chatham House rules. I can tell you, however, that a group of eminent people in the UK energy and electricity worlds sat round the table and discussed, with straight faces, how we were to do this. We had in front of us a briefing paper that made it clear to me that there was no way this aim could be achieved in time and that, when and if ever it was achieved, the costs would be astronomic. Yet the people round the table (I was the sole exception) were purporting to believe that it was do-able.

As Lord Lawson has pointed out, the danger from the standpoint of the UK is that we are the one country in the world that has really decided to buck the trend by intensifying its commitment to cutting back carbon emissions. One of the UK's characteristics – I shall not call it a weakness! – is that we tend to comply with international rules, even if they are so ridiculous that every other country ignores them. I do not believe, on the whole, in failing to fulfil international commitments. In this case, however, the commitment is an extremely foolish one.

This country is now responsible for less than 2% of worldwide carbon dioxide emissions. The idea that cutting down on our emissions may persuade others to do the same is absurd. Whatever they may say, China and India are not going to accept targets that seriously render their economic expansion vulnerable. Why should they? The West has grown prosperous by sensibly using oil and coal, easily the cheapest sources of power. Other nations are not going to be told that they cannot do the same.

So we shall not be achieving anything allegedly ecologically significant by cutting our emissions – but what we shall do is harm ourselves. In fact, we may achieve less than nothing if we are strict with ourselves because, if we make it difficult for people to do business in our country by making it expensive, that business will be exported to those countries where they take less notice of the rules. So there could in fact be more, not less, carbon dioxide emitted.

The fallacy involved in the precautionary principle

This point about displacement of costs is the answer to the so-called precautionary principle. In other words, if the risk of some disaster is not very high, one should, if the potential problem would be very severe, take the necessary steps to prevent it from happening, rather as one may be willing to pay an insurance premium in case one's house burns down. There must, however, be some reasonable correlation between the premium paid and the risk against which one is insuring.

In my opinion the risk against which one might 'insure' is, in the case of global warming, minute. However, even if it were much higher, the idea of today impoverishing millions of the world's people, to an extent that may well lead to many deaths, should be out of the question. It is just too high a premium.

Professor Lord Stern, in a well-known but, I am glad to say, very much criticised, report, suggested that it would cost something like 1% of GDP now to deal with the 'problem', whereas, in 100 years' time, it would, if nothing were done about it at this stage, cost something like 5% of what would then be GDP. That was supposed to be an argument for spending the money now.

If, however, that were in fact true, we ought, on the contrary, to vote in favour of dealing with it in 100 years' time, not now. Why? Because the loss of 1% of GDP now, would, as I have suggested, have a disastrous effect on large numbers of people. In 100 years' time, on the other hand, a reasonably conservative estimate is that the world will be ten times as rich as it is today. So we can very easily indeed – or I should say the people alive in 100 years' time can very easily indeed – afford 5% of the world's vast wealth at that point.

The rapid expansion of human knowledge

I must draw attention to another basis for scepticism to which little attention has been given so far. In 2003 the distinguished economist Roger Bootle made a number of confident predictions that seemed wild at the time.[3] In particular, he said that there would be a major depression caused by a financial collapse, which would be accompanied by huge stock-market losses, major declines in house prices, and so on. He quotes with approval an estimate that the stock of scientific knowledge was in 2003 doubling every five or seven years.

Let us be conservative and assume it takes seven years. Just think what that means if it continues, as he expects that it will. Readers who are good at their powers of 2 will realise that if the sum of knowledge doubles every 7 years it will, in 49 years' time, be 128 times what it is today. In 98 years' time it will be more than 16,000 times what it is today.

It is true that scientific knowledge is not the same as economic progress, but it is certainly linked to it. My point is that, even if the alarmists are right about what they fear would happen if we do nothing to prevent it, it is near enough a certainty that within even 50 years, let alone 100 years, solutions will have been discovered to many of our current or supposed problems. These solutions will be ones of which we cannot even conceive at the moment, just as the internet was beyond our imagination 50 years ago. For me, this is yet another convincing reason why it is madness needlessly to adopt the alarmist stance.

Electric trails

I now conclude on the subject of the CRU emails and hysterical green deceptions in general. Those emails show that the alarmists have been willing to go to extraordinary lengths to convince people of the rightness of their cause. I am very much inclined to think that they, at any rate to start with, did completely believe that they were correct. Yet having once taken up their position, many of them were evidently prepared to go to enormous, and unethical, lengths to convince others that they were right. In defending themselves – or in defending the view that this discovery did not invalidate the global alarmism case – they are apt to make three points, among others:

(1) That the emails were stolen and that that is the main story.

(2) That the science has all been peer reviewed, so there is nothing to discuss.

(3) That this was done only by the Climate Research Unit of the University of East Anglia, and that there are thousands of other scientists who believe in the

hypothesis. Therefore, whatever one thinks about the University of East Anglia, it has virtually no effect on the main theory.

The answers, briefly, are as follows:

(1) The fact that the emails were stolen or leaked does not affect the importance of what they contained. This is so obvious that I shall not dwell on it.

(2) The fact that some scientific theory has been peer reviewed does very little indeed to show that the theory is true, particularly in this case, in which the raw data involved has been lost or thrown away. Peer review merely establishes whether an article is thought sufficiently interesting to be published.

(3) The University of East Anglia Climate Research Unit is regarded all over the world as the leading single measurer of world temperature. The 'thousands of scientists' concerned are not independent of each other. All build on each other's work, and all rely on the temperature data that we now know to be dangerously unreliable. No conspiracy is therefore required for one now to doubt the alarmism.

Following Michael Mann's hockey stick and the CRU emails, came the revelation and apology from the UN's Intergovernmental Panel on Climate Change (the IPCC), the organisation supposed to be the main authority on the subject, about the fact that an important part of their most recent and authoritative 'assessment' was completely wrong and based on a typographical error. Worse still – and, indeed, shocking if true – is the allegation that the chairman of the IPCC, Dr Rajendra K. Pachauri, knew of this but concealed it at the Copenhagen conference in December 2009.

Is global warming the biggest hoax in history?

Honesty is practicality

Finally, there is one practical problem of great importance. The senior politicians in the three main parties have all very strongly committed themselves to the belief that global warming is a major problem. Even if they do begin to realise that actually this is not the case, how are they going to be able to change their stance without being accused of a damaging u-turn? I think the recent very shocking cases of deception can perhaps provide the justification they need – we must certainly hope so.

7.
Earning it back

Politicians should not, where money is concerned, do anything of which, if it came to the knowledge of the public, they would be ashamed. That is the approach that underlies everything else I have said in the most important part of this pamphlet, which deals with MPs' finances. Whether I am demanding a full investigation into every abuse that has happened (even where we may have to accept that shame will be the only penalty) or saying that laws should be enforced by properly constituted courts, the principle is the same. Furthermore, I say that MPs themselves should be obliged to determine their pay, in order that we, the public, can hold them to account.

But I want to stress the enormous obstacles still in the way of reform actually happening, of trust being restored, and of transparency being achieved.

The political class

Labour has created a vast, ever more homogeneous, political class made up of all the main parties. It intends, in practice, to leave it untouched. Many of those who have abused their expenses in the past are set to continue as members of parliament and, of those, a large number will very likely become senior ministers in the next House of Commons. With all three main parties largely as guilty as each other, there is no easy means for the voters to express their feelings about this ongoing scandal if they want to vote for one of the three main parties. I shall conclude by saying what I think the purpose of having MPs should be. My great fear is that what the expenses scandal has all too painfully illuminated is that so many MPs have lost sight of their true role.

MPs dominated by their leaders

I am convinced, however, that whether it is to achieve that essential transparency, or to see MPs rediscover what it means to be a private member, there to serve his or her electors, one thing above all else is necessary: MPs must free themselves from their presently absolute domination by their party leaderships, whom it suited to see MPs reduced to dull dependence. They are opposed to real reform. No wonder: for the system which, until the revelations, they did not intend to change, suited them well.

Transparency essential

We have seen how a flawed system has been covertly still further abused. But the thing to remember about the preceding chapters in this pamphlet, or indeed the avalanche of stories last year is that we were, thank goodness, told about them. By good luck (and considerable journalistic ingenuity) some of what had been happening was disclosed. That is why we must now, as a first step to inoculating ourselves against further abuses, secure as much transparency as possible.

When MPs are provided with generous payments, as salary or allowances, these do not become elevated to some special status. Even so, these payments are not quite like any others. We expect MPs to show a higher standard of trustworthiness and accountability than others.

I have suggested the juridical approach. Open courts will be a deterrent, as well as being the appropriate tribunal to hear cases about alleged abuses. But I do not want us to have to deal again with a system which sharp MPs have an opportunity to exploit. The answer is publicity. As the astute parliamentary sketchwriter, Simon Carr, said of the virtues of publicity in *The Independent*:

> The answer to expenses [is not the IPSA, it is] a wiki-site on the internet. Everything an MP claims for goes up on the site. It will be interrogated by the public, of that we can be sure. Every one of those 5 million receipts will be seen by someone or other, and interesting examples will be forwarded to party leaders and newspapers. This removes the need for...another quango, for a complex bureaucratic structure, for summonses and appeals and interminable consultations. It puts scrutiny in the hands of 'the people'. It devolves power in the way they are always saying they want to do. It involves the public. And the primary deterrent to extravagant or doubtful claims will be cultural, not procedural.[1]

A mishmash of bodies

Instead, as things stand, we are set to inherit the world so bitingly described by Heather Brooke, the woman who started the process by which the truth began to be told. That world avoids clarity in favour of the current system where we still have:

1. The Senior Salaries Review Body (which makes recommendations on MPs' salaries and pensions)

2. The Committee on Standards and Privileges (appointed by the House of Commons to decide on complaints against individual MPs reported to them by the parliamentary commissioner for standards – currently John Lyon)

3. The Committee on Standards in Public Life (which deals with complaints about unethical conduct among MPs – the current chair is Sir Christopher Kelly)

4. The Members Allowances Committee (made up of MPs who advise the Members Estimate Committee on the rules surrounding allowances)

5. The modernisation of the House of Commons Select Committee

6. The Reform of the House of Commons Committee (created to modernise the House in ways presumably more modern than the modernisation of the House of Commons Committee)

7. The Department of Resources (the Fees Office) – previously responsible for paying expense claims

8. To these we can now add IPSA, a Commissioner for Parliamentary Investigations, and a new Speaker's Committee for the IPSA.[2]

The Speaker

All of this is enthusiastically endorsed by Speaker Bercow. For rather than heed the lessons of the past, and learn from where the last Speaker went so badly wrong, Mr Bercow says he sees it as his role to *lead* the Commons in the new direction, not just help them to go there. If he restricted himself to modish interventions in favour of politically correct nostrums about how the House should best be able to represent wider British society, we could leave it at that. But John Bercow is, unfortunately, vastly more influential than merely a noise off: he is central to both the current system and the proposed future one.

Under the terms of the 2009 Parliamentary Standards Act, members of IPSA will be crown appointees – but they will be approved by the Commons following selection by the Speaker 'on the basis of fair and open competition and with the agreement of the Speaker's Committee'. Worse still, having been elected to replace a scapegoat, Speaker Bercow is already casting round for scapegoats of his own. Andrew Walker, the Commons Director of Resources, and the official most exposed on the matter of investigating members' expenses, was very publicly told by Mr Bercow that he would be losing *his* job.

For failing to prevent MPs *like John Bercow* from milking the system they presided over, Mr Walker suffered the indignity of reading, in a magazine interview in December 2009, Mr Bercow say, 'IPSA will be up and running in due course and some staff from the Commons Resources Department will join it – but by no means all. I am not anticipating that the most senior staff from the Resources Department will be joining IPSA. Repeat: I am not anticipating that the senior staff will join'. Real reform of the House of Commons will not, if it comes at all, be led by the member for Buckingham.

Speaker Bercow seems to believe that, for what *he* sees as reform to be credible in the eyes of the public, some sacrificial lambs are required in order to symbolise 'change', the token Clause Four moment so beloved of those products of the new political class on both sides of the House. He no doubt regards his hapless predecessor as just such a necessary victim, sufficient moreover to shut the file marked Speakership. What Mr Bercow cannot, or dare not, see is that his own elevation to the office represents exactly the sort of 'as you were' attitude that would make his swift departure the perfect symbol for which certainly the public and apparently he himself are yearning.

Disclosure by party leaders?

My worry about the future is one reason why I say we should press for reform right now. If complicit MPs can delay reform today, they can reasonably expect to delay it indefinitely. Parliament could learn much from the US Congress. MPs are already getting off lightly by comparison with senators and congressmen, and the gap is likely to increase. In America, the Ethics Reform Act of 1989 obliges Congressmen to file 'Personal Disclosure Reports'. These detail their assets and liabilities, their income (excluding official salaries), asset transactions, gifts, and property where it produces income. Even more exactingly, the source of their spouse's income, assets and liabilities must also be filed, and are available online for their electors to see. While that might be seen as an American solution for American problems, it suggests that nothing I have proposed for MPs is overly onerous.

I do wonder too whether we should, in time for the election, introduce one pertinent aspect of U.S. elections: full financial disclosure for party leaders. This would be unusual but is it not right that party leaders should put some substance behind the *mea culpas* they have uttered? Since all the *Telegraph* was able to reveal was a four year snapshot, why should Brown, Cameron and Clegg not emulate Obama? They have all spoken equally highly of him, and his approach to politics; why should they not copy his approach to fighting elections as a party leader? He gave a full, lifetime financial disclosure, detailing his, and his wife's, income from sources private and public. Why could our party leaders not give a parliamentary equivalent, detailing all public allowances and other benefits each of them has obtained since he entered the Commons? If they decline to do so I would say 'I wonder why?'.

Conservatives prepared to do more than Labour?

If the current Speaker is distinctly uninspiring, as far as restoring trust is concerned, the probable next Prime Minister, David Cameron, does not really inspire more confidence than Gordon Brown. He said recently, 'There is no chance Gordon Brown will do what is right and put the public interest before his own political interest'. I fear that is true – but what about himself?

At the root of his praised handling of the crisis on behalf of the Conservative party was Cameron's tactic to apologise and move on. This was not 'apologise, repent and punish' but, in essence, just a media handling technique. It was a good example of the response of the political class to the expenses scandal. Surprising as it will one day seem, MPs across the House appear to believe that, having been exposed for claiming expenses they now say they should not have had, they are nevertheless adequately punished by merely being required to hand those expenses back.

We should not be surprised. David Cameron no more sought to reform the system than Mr Brown did, until he was forced to do so by the press revelations. Moreover, as much as any New Labour politician, he is a product of the discredited system. What do all these roles discharged by him have in common: being an MP; being Leader of the Opposition; being a Special Advisor; even working in the Conservative Research Department (CRD)? All of them, either directly, or indirectly, have meant he has been throughout most of his working life in receipt of a publicly funded salary. He is unlikely to be a radical.

David Cameron was clever in the way he presented his response to the crisis. At its height last summer, the Leader of the Opposition declared, 'it is information – not a new law, not some new regulation – just the provision of information that has enabled people to take on the political class, question them, demand answers, and get those answers'. What does that really mean? Does he intend to tell us everything he already knows, such as, if indeed he does know them, the tax details about Lord Ashcroft which have frequently been sought?

The Tory leader enjoys the benefit of the Parliamentary Resources Unit (PRU). This, in practice financed by a tithe of most Conservative MPs (or to be more precise, by a tithing of their publicly provided allowances), exists nominally to provide an aggregate 'research' facility for Conservative MPs, though in effect it displaces much of the function previously provided for by CRD.

In its evidence to *Kelly*, the PRU disavowed any 'political activity'.[3] Yet it is run by Conservative appointees, it serves only Tory MPs, and no staff member gets hired without the say-so of the shadow ministerial team. The party's chief whip is the leading figure in its administration, and its work is closely integrated with that of both the Leader's Office and CCHQ.

At one of *Kelly's* public hearings, Kevin Flack observed that the PRU 'provides the parliamentary research and support to the main opposition party'.[4] Unquestionably the party takes briefing materials from it. Yet the funding mechanism of the PRU – a slice of MPs' allowances 'volunteered' by them – is meant to forbid it from being anything like a publicly supported research arm of the Conservative party machine. No one knows better than the Leader of the Opposition what the PRU is actually doing for his party, but what information does he provide?

Then there is Short Money. Despite the fact that in the last year alone the Conservative party received more that £4 million worth of this public subsidy (and a further £650,000 for the Leader of the Opposition's private office), what information does Cameron provide about this? He does what the law requires him to do and no more. He provides the Clerk of the Commons (the accounting officer for these funds) with an auditor's certificate confirming that 'all expenses claimed were incurred exclusively in relation to the party's parliamentary business'. That is it: nothing else. The certificate gives no details at all about these activities.

Is this a system in which David Cameron would have confidence if it were supposed to monitor some other body receiving the better part of £5 million annually? Does his absolute lack of disclosure about what he is doing with this money tally with his declarations about 'the provision of information' and what it can achieve? Why, in short, does he not provide *any* information here? This silence is one reason why I wish I could have more confidence that he intends to reform the parliamentary expenses system.

Yet even if Cameron were strongly committed to restoring trust in parliament, even if he had shown himself to be a champion of that cause and determined to see it through, regardless of personal or party cost, would he be able to? The Conservative Leader has accepted much of what he calls the 'Blairite system', and explicitly commended himself for doing so. Thatcher ripped up unsatisfactory systems. Potential Prime Minister Cameron, on the other hand, appears to accept the very thing that will make any attempt at genuine reform more or less impossible to achieve. He proposes to leave firmly in place the vast, salaried political class

New Labour has brought into being. Whatever he himself thinks about reform, this class will never attack the culture that brought it into existence and keeps it well rewarded.

Overpayment of all politicians

Cameron's pledge to reduce the number of MPs by a tenth is fine, but it does not deal with this problem. The problem has many symptoms, but one common cause: the enormous overpayment of politicians since 1997 for which New Labour is responsible. When organisations like the TaxPayers' Alliance ask pertinent questions about huge public sector benefits, this is the real point: has it been necessary? What, after all, constituted a 'going rate'? Let us leave MPs to one side, as there is never any lack of would-be MPs. Who can say that we are paying council chief executives, for example, a sane rate? Are they demonstrably delivering better productivity, improved services, or lower costs, let alone cheaper council tax bills?

The BBC is another example: it has been forced, at last, to let the National Audit Office investigate it. Its top one hundred salaried employees get paid £20 million. Why? What is the competition to the BBC in the areas where it operates, and is mostly dominant? Though Jeremy Paxman is a wonderful example of a type, I do doubt whether a private competitor nowadays would match the income the public hands over to him. As I say, while these are each a different question, their answers come to the same: the vast inflation of political salaries. For why would politicians prevent civil servants, local government officials or anyone else on the public payroll from inflating their salaries, if that risked a cut-back on the payments they too now received?

The figures speak for themselves. The cost for *national and devolved* politicians in 2007/8 was stated (by the BBC itself!) as follows: MPs' and ministers' pay plus their Commons staff, expenses and allowances, policy development grants and Short Money £167 million; salaries, expenses and payments to the opposition in the Lords approximately £19.1 million; in Whitehall, up to 73 special advisers approximately £5.9m; the Scottish parliament £19 million, the Welsh Assembly, £10.3 million, and, the Northern Ireland Assembly £13.3 million; London's Mayor and Assembly £5.4 million; and finally, for how could we forget them, while British MEPs' salaries formally cost £4,821,960, the European parliament would not disclose the total bill for their expenses and other costs. All the devolved tiers are New Labour innovations. But this is dwarfed by the gigantic cost of councillors in modern Britain. There are 22,737 and, with their ever more plentiful assistants, they cost £254.6 million in 2007/8.

Local councillors now have a stake in their parties far greater than ever before, because the parties now have ever more say in whether they can be councillors in the first place. All this has happened since the Local Government Act in 2000 swept away the traditional, and cost-effective, committee system of administration, and replaced it with an 'executive' one, mostly with 'cabinets' and indirectly elected leaders (though there have also been up to a dozen directly elected mayors). The cost of local government has increased exponentially.

The most recent figures (June 2009) from the Local Government Association (the LGA – effectively the trade union for councils, controlled at the moment by Conservative councillors) show the shocking extent of this problem. The average basic allowance for all councillors is just over £6,000. Remember that this is up from almost nothing, bar minimal expenses. In London the average councillor salary is almost £10,000. For council leaders, the average in London is almost £40,000. The average leader's allowance nationally is £17,753. For 'cabinet' or 'executive' members, the average allowance is £9,710, and cabinet/executives generally have ten members. 'Chairs of overview and scrutiny' receive an average allowance of £6,136, with the average number of such posts in each authority being 2.6; chairs of planning committees receive an average allowance of £5,623 and chairs of licensing committees an average of £4,334.

We were democratic long before this wave of public money flooded into the system. But my worry is how democratic we are going to be now. Councillors are routinely voting themselves inflation busting, recession defying, pay rises. Many of them are cynically conscious of the fact that individual councils are usually not elected for their individual merit, but on what the voters think of their parties. National media coverage of council elections centres on what the national parties are doing centrally, rather than what the councils in question have done *locally*. For councillors, this means that they are judged by the voters not on what they have done themselves but, all too often, on how their party is perceived to have performed nationally. This further distances councillors from any proper and direct sense of local accountability.

Labour responsible for current situation

Labour is mainly to blame for this. They introduced the complex, costly, yet ineffective Electoral Commission; it is Labour which has presided over the pay and allowances of an enormous political class; it is Labour whose pettiness has led them to choose an unfit Speaker and stand by him until he self-destructed; and who foisted on the Commons a man with no respect for its traditions, and who is personally mired in the crisis that destroyed his predecessor. Labour's foes might in 1997 have suspected them of a lack of reverence for British political traditions, but few would at that time have been pessimistic enough to predict all this. David Cameron's tragedy is that there seems to be no area where he proposes real change, nor even one instance where he, and those who come in his wake, will do anything more than more of the same.

No real punishment

What in the end have the MPs who have let the country down suffered for what they have done?

Four MPs are to be punished, but is that really to be all? Vague talk of 'parliament's good name' obscures just how great the escape from responsibility has been. The cry that 'we're all guilty' really amounts to: 'none of us is, individually'. I fear that we are heading for Marie Antoinette politics. We have a Bourbon opposition that has learned very little from the worst parliamentary scandal in British democratic history, but has, as a clique, forgotten nothing in pursuit of factional advantage.

What are MPs for? To be a tally in their leader's back pocket for the purpose of parliamentary divisions? We may as well in that case do away with them, and just give the party leaders whatever percentage score 'they' get at general elections. The leaders could be like trade union barons of old, waving their cards at TUC conferences. Perhaps MPs are necessary just to provide party leaders with a cadre of shadow or actual ministerial frontbenchers? Why bother with MPs at all then? Why not simply do what France or America or the EU does and have all or most or many ministers entirely unelected?

The case for having MPs at all is that they are there to test the executive. To do this, we need MPs who do not see being in parliament as a career, who do not see life in the Commons as merely an extension of life in civil service with added television appearances, and who see virtue in being independent of their parties, in being able to exercise their own judgement, and in not being beholden for their livelihoods to their party leaders. These are the MPs whom we can trust to give their first allegiance to their constituents. Please let us have more like them.

References

Chapter 1.
1. 12th Report, Committee on Standards in Public Life, Cm 7724, hereafter *Kelly*
2. Robert Winnett & Gordon Rayner, *No Expenses Spared*, Bantam Press, 2009, hereafter *NEP*
3. On this theme, see more generally the research of Dr Jason Peacey in John Adamson (ed.) *The English Civil War: Conflict and Contexts* (London, 2009)
4. Clement Walker, *Relations*, p143; Mercurius Pragmaticus, no.38 (12-19 Dec. 1648), sig. Ddd.
5. Walker, *Relations*, pp1-3
6. G. S., *A Letter from an Ejected Member* (1648), p10
7. HC Deb 10 August 1911 c1383
8. Review body on top salaries, 1st report: Ministers of the Crown and Members of Parliament, 1971-72 Cm 4836; hereafter *Boyle*
9. *Boyle*, ch 4, p14, par 40; my italics
10. HC Deb 20 December 1971 vol 828, c1134

Chapter 2.
1. *Kelly*, public hearings, 23 June 09, par48/9
2. *NES*, p102
3. *NES*, p303
4. The Spectator's 'Coffee House', 10 May 2009, 10.43pm, http://www.spectator.co.uk/coffeehouse/3604396/gove-the-full-story.thtml
5. *NES*, p174
6. *Camberley News & Mail*, 19 May 2009
7. *The Guardian*, 19 May 2009
8. House of Commons library: Parliamentary Trends: Statistics about Parliament (RESEARCH PAPER 09/69 12 August 2009), p53
9. *The Times*, 16 May 09

Chapter 3.
1. *Kelly*, Recommendation 20
2. *Kelly*, Recommendation 60
3. *Kelly* 7724, p10
4. *Kelly*, p67, 8.3
5. *Kelly*, p10
6. *Kelly* 7724, p11
7. *Kelly*, Recommendation 16
8. House of Commons Library, PSB 09/61
9. *Kelly*, PH 7 July 2009, par42
10. *Kelly*, p103, 13.43
11. *Kelly*, p28, 1.8

Chapter 6.
1. Duckworth Overlook, 2008
2. Ibid., p107
3. *Money for Nothing* (Nicholas Brealey Publishing, 2003)

Chapter 7.
1. *The Independent*, 22nd June 2009
2. *The Guardian*, 10th December 2009